Canadian Battlefields 1915-1918
A Visitor's Guide

Terry Copp
Matt Symes
Nick Lachance

LCMSDS Press/Wilfrid Laurier University Press

0 1 2 3 4 5 6 7 8 9

Printed in Canada

Library and Archives Canada Cataloguing in Publication
Copp, Terry, 1938-
    Canadian battlefields 1915-1918 : a visitor's guide / Terry Copp, Matt Symes, Nick Lachance.

Includes bibliographical references.
ISBN 978-1-926804-11-8

    1. World War, 1914-1918--Battlefields--France--Guidebooks. 2. World War, 1914-1918--Battlefields--Belgium--Guidebooks. 3. World War, 1914-1918--Campaigns--Western Front. 4. Canada. Canadian Army--History--World War, 1914-1918. I. Symes, Matt, 1980- II. Lachance, Nick, 1982- III. Laurier Centre for Military, Strategic and Disarmament Studies IV. Title.

D528.C67 2011   940.4'144   C2011-906137-6

Printed and bound in Canada
Design: Matt Symes with Nick Lachance
Cover Photograph: Matt Symes
Distributed by: Wilfrid Laurier University Press/University of Toronto Press
Laurier Centre for Military Strategic and Disarmament Studies
www.canadianmilitaryhistory.ca

Table of Contents

This visitor's guide to the Canadian battlefields on the Western Front 1915-1918 completes the series of guidebooks, published by the Laurier Centre for Military, Strategic and Disarmament Studies (LCMSDS), to the Canadian battlefields in Europe. Our first titles, originally published in 1994-1995 for the 50th anniversaries of the Normandy invasion and the end of the war, have gone through several editions and revisions which eliminated chapters on the First World War in favour of an in-depth treatment of the 1944-1945 campaign in Northwest Europe. We now present a user-friendly guide to the Canadian experience on the Great War battlefields in Belgium and France.

This book is not intended as an exhaustive review of battles or battlefields. We have selected events and tour itineraries on the basis of fifteen years of experience leading study tours for university students, high school teachers and the general public. We have highlighted the most important books and websites to encourage further readings but most visitors will find that the guidebook provides enough information to allow for a basic understanding of what happened and why it happened that way.

Terry Copp wrote the history and is responsible for errors, omissions, and interpretive judgements. His students and colleagues at Wilfrid Laurier University and l'Université de Montréal and especially those who have participated in the "Cleghorn Battlefield Tours" have provided the opportunity to test out ideas and advance understanding of the war experience. Mike Bechthold, Geoff Hayes, Mark Humphries, Andrew Iarocci, Carl Bouchard, Michel Fortmann, Geoff Keelan, Caitlin McWilliams, and his students in History 360 during the fall of 2010 deserve special thanks.

Terry Copp, Matt Symes and Nick Lachance wrote the tour section. Matt Symes had overall responsibility for the book design. Nick Lachance worked with Google Earth images to create the battle and tour maps while Mike Bechthold developed the overview maps. Most of the modern day photos were taken by Nick Lachance and Matt Symes on the 2009 and 2010 Cleghorn Study Tour as well as the 2011 War and Memory Class. Eric McGeer and Brandey Barton were gracious enough to edit various versions of the guide. Eric's guidance with the appendices, suggestions for war art, as well as the modern day photos he contributed have added immensely to the final product. Brendan O'Driscoll, Caleb Burney, Mike Lakusiak and Jordan Burrows helped with editing the final draft. Elise De Garie checked the text for the proper French translations and helped with the design of the cover. As he often does, Geoff Keelan acted as our last line of defence in the editing process and his keen eye allowed us to avoid some embarrassing mistakes.

Our long-standing partnership with the Canadian War Museum (CWM), and especially Susan Ross and Laura Brandon, has allowed us to incorporate some of the outstanding war art from the First World War which has greatly enhanced the final product. Where you see CWM in the caption, this refers to the Beaverbrook Collection of War Art held at the Canadian War Museum. Every effort has been made to give proper reference to the illustrations we have used. We are grateful to Google for permission to use their copyright imagery to illustrate the battlefields.

We welcome comments, suggestions and questions: tcopp@wlu.ca, matt. symes@symplicity.ca, or lachance.nicholas@gmail.com.

Mary Riter Hamilton, *Dug Out on the Somme*. [LAC 1988-180-3]

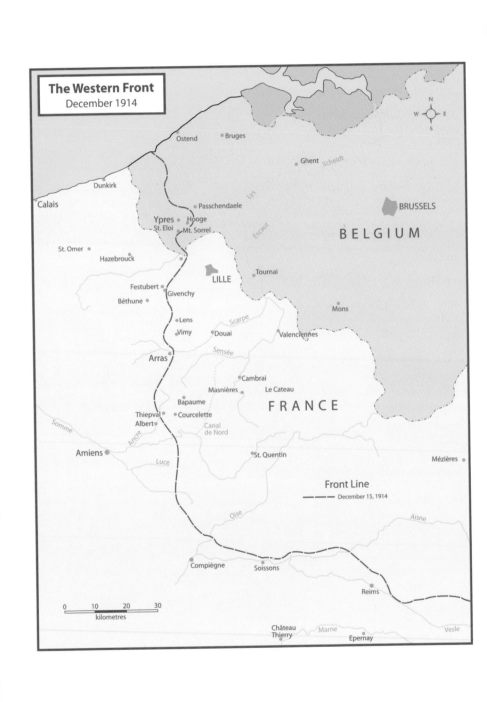

The Western Front
December 1914

N
W E
S

Ostend · Bruges

Ghent · Scheldt

Dunkirk

Calais

· Passchendaele

BRUSSELS

Ypres · Hooge
· St. Eloi · Mt. Sorrel

BELGIUM

St. Omer ·

Hazebrouck

LILLE

Tournai

Festubert ·
Béthune · Givenchy

Mons

· Lens

Scarpe

· Vimy · Douai

Valenciennes

Arras

Sensée

Cambrai

Masnières · Le Cateau

FRANCE

Bapaume

Thiepval · · Courcelette
Albert ·

Canal de Nord

Somme

Ancre

Amiens ·

Luce

· St. Quentin

Mézières ·

Front Line
— — — December 15, 1914

Oise

Aisne

Compiègne · Soissons

Reims

0   10   20   30
kilometres

Château
Thierry   Marne   Vesle

Epernay

Lys

Escaut

Canada at War

M ost of the world remembers the First World War as a time when "innocent young men, their heads full of high abstractions like Honour, Glory and England...were slaughtered in stupid battles planned by stupid Generals." English-speaking Canadians, while generally accepting this view, have supplemented it with an imaginative version of a war in which their soldiers won great victories and forged a new national identity. Both of these approaches have served to promote literary, political and cultural agendas of such power that empirical studies of what actually happened during the war have had little impact upon the historiography. Recently, a new generation of scholars have challenged this approach, insisting that "the reality of the war and the society which produced it" are also worthy of study. If historians are to continue to study the past to further understand what happened, and why it happened that way, they need to remember that the men and women who participated in events like the First World War were not concerned with the views of later generations. The meaning of their war was constantly changing and since no one knew the outcome, or the consequences, of decisions which needed to be made they relied upon the best information available at the time and tried to act in ways that did not violate their shared values.

It is clear, for example, that while Canadians were surprised that the assassination of an Austrian archduke should lead to war, those citizens interested in world affairs had long been aware of the possibility of such a conflict. The enmity between Germany and France, the alliance system, and the increasingly bitter rivalry of the German and British Empires were topics of informed discussion throughout most of the decade that preceded the war. The "naval question" along with reciprocity or free trade with the United States, dominated pre-war political debate and sensitized many of those normally indifferent to such topics. Canadians were divided on issues of war and peace and especially divided on military and naval expenditure precisely because they thought they understood what was at stake.

French Canadian opinion, at least within Quebec, was almost universally opposed to any form of military expenditure that might underwrite Canadian participation in foreign wars. Within English-speaking Canada there were sharp divisions between Imperialists, Canadian Nationalists, anti-militarists and declared pacifists. While newspapers like the *Montreal Star* and the *Toronto Mail and Empire* offered strong support for military preparedness, the *Toronto Globe*, the

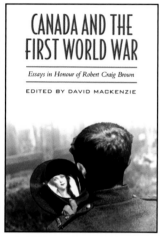

Methodist Guardian and the voice of the western farmer, *The Grain Growers Guide*, were equally adamant about the dangers of militarism. David Mackenzie has edited a collection of essays, *Canada and the First World War*, which touches on these and other key issues.

Canada's leaders played no part in the decision for war in 1914 and it is literally true that Canada went to war because Britain was at war. This statement, while accurate, does little to help us make sense of the events of August 1914 in Europe or in Canada. To achieve understanding we must answer three different questions: (1) Who was believed to be responsible for the outbreak of war? (2) Why was Britain involved? (3) What kind of war was it going to be? The answers to these questions seemed obvious to Canadians. Germany was threatening the peace of Europe and violating Belgian neutrality as part of an attack on France. Britain was defending France against German aggression and coming to the assistance of Belgium. The war was likely to be over by Christmas after decisive battles between standing armies, but it might last until 1915.

The response of most English-speaking Canadians was predictable. Canada was part of the Empire and must actively support the mother country in a just war which Britain had tried to prevent. This view of the origins of the war was dismissed as simplistic in the 1920s when historians developed a revisionist interpretation which ignored evidence of German intentions. Today the scholarly consensus presents a picture not very different from the one accepted by Canadians in 1914. Two of the most interesting essay collections on the origins of the war are Keith

Wilson, *Decisions for War 1914*, and Holger Afflerbach and David Stevenson, *An Improbable War*.

The country's commitment to the war effort was not in doubt but Canada could not provide any immediate assistance. Wilfrid Laurier's attempt to create a Canadian Navy, able to defend Canada's coasts and assist in the protection of imperial sea lanes, ended with his defeat in 1911. The Liberal-controlled Senate then blocked Prime Minister Robert Borden's Naval Aid Bill which offered direct financial assistance to the Royal Navy. As a result, in 1914 the Royal Canadian Navy possessed one seaworthy, if obsolescent, light cruiser, *HMCS Rainbow* and two submarines hastily purchased from the neutral United States by the government of British Columbia.

Canada's regular army of 3,000 all ranks as well as some 70,000 volunteers serving in the militia was a far more considerable force than the navy. Under the energetic if eccentric leadership of Sam Hughes, Minister of Militia since 1911, fifty-six new armouries and drill halls were built and training camps created or expanded. Hughes is usually remembered for his misguided commitment to the Ross Rifle, a Canadian-designed and manufactured weapon, which proved deficient under combat conditions. But if Hughes is to be condemned for his errors of judgement, he must also be remembered for encouraging more realistic training, marksmanship, the acquisition of modern guns for the artillery, and

the expansion of the militia. Ronald Haycock's biography *Sam Hughes*, published in 1986, is still the basic source for Hughes' career, but Tim Cook's 2010 book *The Madman and the Butcher* provides a well-written account of Hughes as well as his conflict with Arthur Currie.

Whatever view one takes of Hughes, it is evident that no Canadian field force could possibly have gone into action on a European battlefield in 1914. This did not stop the Minister from trying. On 6 August he sent 226 night telegrams directly to unit commanders of the militia ordering them to interview prospective recruits and wire lists of volunteers for overseas service to Ottawa. Hughes bypassed existing mobilization plans and required that the Canadian Expeditionary Force (CEF) to assemble at a new, yet to be built, embarkation camp at Valcartier near Quebec City.

Would the original plan have worked more smoothly? Would a conventionally recruited force of 30,000 men have been ready to leave for England in October? We will never know but it is impossible not to be impressed with what Hughes and William Price, who created Valcartier Camp and organized the embarkation of troops, accomplished in just seven weeks.

One legacy of Hughes' decision to scrap the mobilization scheme was the failure to designate a French-Canadian battalion in what was to become the First Canadian Division. French-speaking recruits were shunted to the 14th Battalion (Royal Montreal Regiment) where they joined two of the four companies in a unit where English was the dominant language. The Maritime provinces were also excluded from representation in the new numbered battalions of the CEF. Given the apparent support for the war that was evident in Quebec in 1914 when even Henri Bourassa, the *nationaliste* icon, briefly supported Canadian participation, the absence of a French-Canadian battalion until the 22nd (the "Van Doos") went into action in 1916 did not help recruiting in Quebec.

Who were the men who volunteered to go to war in 1914? Desmond

Morton suggests that "for the most part, the crowds of men who jammed into the armouries were neither militia nor Canadian-born." Most, he argues, were recent British immigrants anxious to return to their homeland in a time of crisis, especially when Canada was deep in a recession which had created large-scale unemployment. Morton's book *When Your Number's Up* is highly recommended. The best available statistics suggest that two thirds of the First Contingent "were British born and bred." Command of the First Division went to a British officer, Lieutenant-General Sir Edwin Alderson, but Hughes appointed Canadians to command the brigades, battalions, and artillery regiments. Much the same pattern held for the Second Contingent. Sixty percent were British-born but their officers were Canadian.

Newfoundlanders were still mourning the loss of more than 300 fishermen in a spring blizzard when news of the war reached the colony. The response was nevertheless enthusiastic and in the absence of a recent British immigrant population, recruits were drawn from a cross section of town and outport communities. Less than a quarter million people lived in Newfoundland in 1914 but thousands volunteered to serve in the Newfoundland Regiment and the Royal Navy. Imperial ties were no doubt basic to this response but many were drawn to serve by the promise of decent pay and a meaningful role in a just war which could not be much more dangerous than the sea.

The men who gathered at Valcartier were supposed to be at least 5'3" tall with a chest measurement of 33.5 inches, between 18 and 45 years of age, and ready to serve for one year "or until the war ended if longer than that." Officers received from $6.50 a day for a Lieutenant-Colonel to $3.60 for a Lieutenant. Non-commissioned officers could earn as much as $2.30 a day while the basic rate for a soldier was $1.10. The Canadian Patriotic Fund soon provided additional support for families from private donations. The Fund, with chapters across Canada, offered support only after investigating the recipients and then provided assistance on a sliding scale which paralleled the army's rates of pay. Desmond Morton's *Fight or Pay* tells the story of the Patriotic Fund. A dollar a day was not far below the income of a junior clerk or unskilled labourer and far above the cash paid to a farm worker. The army was thus an attractive proposition to many

VALCARTIER—BRIG.-GEN. SIR SAM. HUGHES INSPECTING INSTRUCTIONAL STAFF

single men seeking escape from the dull routines of work or the harsh experience of unemployment. A large number of married men also volunteered but Sam Hughes, who insisted participation had to be voluntary in every sense of the word, decided that "no recruit would be accepted against the written protest of his wife or mother." Newspapers reported that "long lists of men were struck off the rolls" because of this regulation.

As the Canadian Expeditionary Force and the Newfoundland Regiment departed for England, a Second Contingent, which would become the Second Canadian Division, was authorized. This decision on 7 October was made in the context of the German advance on Paris, the dramatic retreat of the British Expeditionary Force from Mons, and the miracle of the Battle of the Marne which saved France from immediate defeat. If the war was seen as a romantic adventure in early August, by October the harsh reality of high casualties and the prospect of a German victory now created a more realistic view.

By October, Canadian opinion was also deeply affected by the plight of the Belgian people. Voluntary organizations including farm groups, churches and ad hoc committees responded with offers of money, food, clothing and plans to aid Belgian orphans and refugees. This spontaneous outpouring of sympathy preceded the first atrocity stories which served to further intensify anti-German sentiments and public support for participation in a just war.

England and France 1915

The First Contingent arrived in Britain on 14 October and reached their tented camp on Salisbury Plain near Stonehenge just in time for the worst, wettest winter in recent memory. Over the next four months the contingent trained and equipped itself to join the British Army in Flanders as a standard infantry division of 18,000 men. The establishment included three brigades each of 130 officers, 4,000 men and 272 horses. Each brigade contained four infantry battalions of approximately 900 men commanded by a lieutenant-colonel. A battalion was made up of four rifle companies, each divided into four platoons. Additional firepower was provided by two sections of two Colt machine guns per battalion. The three divisional artillery brigades, equipped with modern eighteen-pounder field guns, provided the firepower that was supposed to permit troops to assault enemy positions neutralized by shelling.

There is no consensus among historians as to how well-prepared the Canadians were when they entered the line in March 1915. Desmond Morton describes the Canadians as "woefully unready." John Swettenham, the author of *To Seize the Victory*, still a very useful survey of the Canadian military effort, emphasized the problems of the Ross Rifle and other difficulties with equipment. Bill Rawling's important study, *Surviving Trench Warfare: Technology and the Canadian Corps 1914-1918*, reminds us that "the Canadian artillery was not able to fire its guns

Men of the First Canadian Contingent march past Stonehenge, autumn 1915. [PA 117875]

until the end of January 1915 and then was allotted just 50 rounds per battery." "The gunners," he writes, "would have to wait until the move to France to gain any real experience with the tools of their trade." Rawling concludes that the First Division was "hardly a well-trained formation," but notes that trench warfare was new to the "professional armies of Europe as well." The official history, G.W.L. Nicholson's *Canadian Expeditionary Force, 1914-19*, quotes the commander of the British Expeditionary Force, Field Marshal Sir John French who reported that the Canadians were "well trained and quite able to take their places in the line." This is the sort of thing generals are required to say and has little other value.

Andrew Iarocci's important study of the training and initial battle experience of First Canadian Division, *Shoestring Soldiers*, presents a detailed analysis of the preparatory period. He argues convincingly that "the Canadians who landed in France in February 1915 were well prepared for battle by contemporary standards." Once in Belgium, they were paired with veteran British battalions, rotated through the trenches and exposed to repeated exercises in rapid fire, fire control and close combat drill. "Every infantry soldier in the division had an opportunity to visit the front lines and work with a British 'buddy' before regrouping into his own platoon for a stint in the trenches."

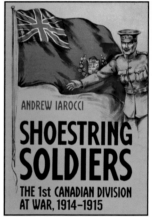

The divisional artillery was also attached to British units and officers went forward to observe the guns in action and to give Canadian FOOs (Forward Observation Officers) "many helpful hints." The importance of camouflaging gun positions was stressed and courses on technical matters were pursued. Captain H.D.G. "Harry" Crerar expressed a common opinion when he wrote, "I'm sure the Canadian Division will do as well as the rest of them for they have the right spirit ... and their training by this time is pretty well completed to the standard of Imperial troops."

In early March 1915, the Canadians took over 6,400 yards of trenches near Armentières close to the Franco-Belgian border. Their first task was to improve the trench defences, a job for the divisional engineer field companies. The First

Brigade Canadian Field Artillery located its batteries of eighteen-pounders near Fleurbaix while the First Canadian Heavy Battery set up positions further back. The front line was at the foot of the Aubers Ridge, a position which provided the Germans with an overview of the Allied lines.

The Canadians and two British divisions were part of 4th Corps, First British Army. The Corps commander Lieutenant-General H.S. Rawlinson was responsible for planning the attack on Neuve Chapelle, the first British offensive of 1915. While the 7th and 8th British Division and the Indian Army Corps captured the village, the Canadian Division was to "maintain its position" and "open artillery, rifle and Maxim gun fire on their immediate front and Fromelles village in order to hold the enemy to his ground and prevent reinforcements being sent to Aubers."

Rawlinson was reasonably confident that his Corps could capture Neuve Chapelle which was in a small salient on the low ground but he believed that General Douglas Haig, the Army Commander, was wildly optimistic about the chance of securing the ridge. Both Haig and Rawlinson knew that the limited amount of artillery shells and shortages in small arms ammunition would limit any advance even if the enemy defences proved to be weak.

Neuve Chapelle was taken but no further advance onto the ridge proved possible. This modest achievement was hailed as a victory despite the 13,000 British and Indian casualties. The Canadians had played their supporting role suffering about a hundred casualties from enemy shelling.

Edgar Bundy, *Landing of the First Canadian Division at Saint-Nazaire.* [CWM 1971061-0110]

Battle of Second Ypres - 22-24 April 1915

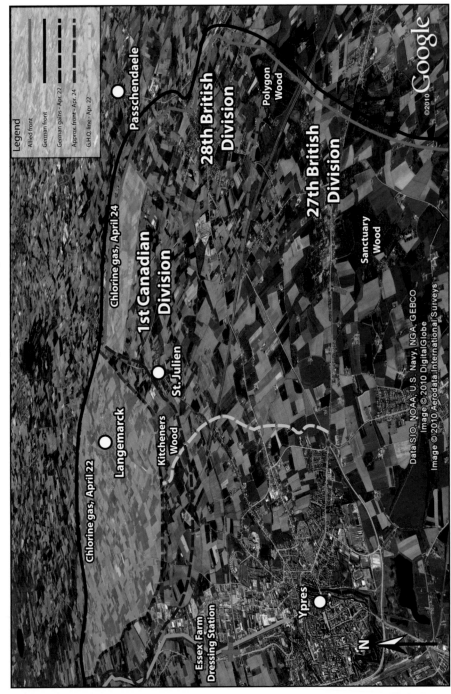

Legend
- Allied front
- German front
- German gains - Apr. 22
- Approx. front - Apr. 24
- G.H.Q. line - Apr. 22

Passchendaele

Chlorine gas, April 24

28th British Division

Polygon Wood

1st Canadian Division

27th British Division

St. Julien

Sanctuary Wood

Kitcheners Wood

Langemarck

Chlorine gas, April 22

Essex Farm Dressing Station

Ypres

N

Data SIO, NOAA, U.S. Navy, NGA, GEBCO
Image © 2010 DigitalGlobe
Image © 2010 Aerodata International Surveys

Google ©2010

Flanders Fields 1915-1916

On 24 March 1915, General Joseph Joffre asked Field Marshal Sir John French to take over parts of the Ypres Salient held by the French Army. This, Joffre argued, would allow his armies to mount a new offensive with adequate reserves. Three divisions, including First Canadian, were transferred to Second British Army with the Canadians joining 5th British Corps in the centre of the salient, adjacent to the remaining French troops.

The 5th British Corps was commanded by Herbert Plumer who later became one of the most cautious and meticulous generals serving on the Western Front. There is little evidence of this approach to combat in April 1915. As the Canadians prepared to take over positions at the apex of the salient, Plumer's first communication was "A Memorandum on Offensive Action" ordering Alderson and his subordinate commanders to make "definite plans" as to where an offensive action "should be carried out." This missive ignored the real problem: the condition of the exposed trenches previously occupied by the 112th French Division.

Cyril Barraud, *First Glimpse of Ypres.* [CWM 19710261-0021]

A view of the deep trench system that had come into being by 1916. [IWM 1900-13]

A "Report on the Condition of the Trenches" prepared by Captain T. C. Irving of the Canadian Engineers noted that, "we found on our arrival conditions to be extremely bad." One section some 1,650 yards long "consisted of 15 isolated portions of trench… The water level is about two feet down below the surface of the ground with numerous shell holes and also a section of the trench behind partially filled with water...In front of these sections are numerous bodies in a decomposed state lying on the surface of the ground..." Most trenches had breastworks made of "heaps of mud" that provided little protection. Frequently further digging uncovered hastily buried bodies from the earlier battles for Ypres. Canadian engineers worked to improve the defences and drain parts of the line but not much could be accomplished in the few days available before the enemy offensive began.

Several credible reports on German plans to attack the salient perhaps employing an asphyxiating gas, led 5th Corps to develop plans for a withdrawal "if it becomes necessary to clear troops out of Ypres" but no redeployment of forward infantry battalions was ordered nor was energy focused on improving the main fall-back position, known as the GHQ Line.

After Neuve Chapelle and a French Army attack in Champagne, which General Joffre insisted was a success because the Germans had to use troops "drawn from other parts of the line" to stop it, both the French and British armies planned to launch new offensives in late April or early May. The Germans, who had been forced to transfer troops to the east to assist the Austro-Hungarian armies, decided to mount an attack to disguise their weakness in the west and to demonstrate their continuing capacity to take the initiative. The German view of Second Ypres is outlined in *Germany's Western Front 1915*, the new

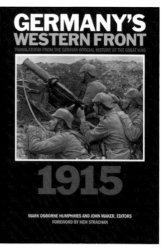

translation of the German official history edited by Mark Humphries and John Maker.

Attempting to collapse the Ypres Salient by an attack from the north was an obvious possibility. As an added bonus, the direction of attack provided a good opportunity to try out a new weapon: chlorine gas. The German Army's experiment with chlorine gas as a method of breaking the stalemate on the Western Front has been re-examined by Tim Cook in his book *No Place to Run*. The Canadians were, he reminds us, sent into a salient which "protruded into the Germans lines like a rounded tumour, eight

miles wide and six miles deep." The positions they took over from the French covered 4,500 yards north of Gravenstafel Ridge and were overlooked by German observers on Passchendaele Ridge to the east.

Eight days after their tour of duty began a period of quiet settled over the salient broken by an intense artillery barrage beginning in the late afternoon. "Along with the shells came an ominous grey-green cloud four miles long and half a mile deep." The gas crept upon the 45th Algerian and 87th French Divisions:

> One by one the French guns fell silent only to be replaced by screaming choking Algerians running into and past the Canadian lines…The victims

of the gas attack writhed on the ground. Their bodies turned a strange gas-green as they struggled to suck oxygen into their corrupted lungs. The chlorine attacked the bronchial tubes, which caused the membranes to swell into a spongy mass and ever-increasing amounts of fluid to enter from the bloodstream. The swiftly congested lungs failed to take in oxygen, and the victims suffocated as they drowned in their own fluids.

The 13th Battalion (Royal Highlanders of Canada) together with two Algerian battalions that were spared all but the edges of the gas cloud created a new defensive line along the Ypres – Poelcappelle road. That evening, French reserves tried to stem the tide of the German advance with a counterattack towards Pilckem Ridge. This attack and the one launched by the 10th (Alberta) and 16th (Canadian Scottish) Battalions to retake Kitcheners Wood just before midnight are regarded as costly failures in win-lose accounts of the war, but both actions served to check the momentum of the German advance.

Early on the morning of 24 April, as the Canadians and the first British reinforcements struggled to build new defensive positions, a second gas attack began. The 15th and 8th Battalions of Canada's Second Brigade, holding the original lines in what was now the apex of the salient, saw the gas drifting towards

Alfred Bastien, *Gas Attack, Flanders*, 1915. [CWM 19710261-0084]

them and urged each other to "piss on your handkerchiefs and tie them over your faces." Urine, the chemistry students in the army recalled, contained ammonia which might neutralize the chlorine. Cook quotes Major Harold Matthews' vivid memories of the moment:

> It is impossible for me to give a real idea of the terror and horror spread among us by the filthy loathsome pestilence. It was not, I think, the fear of death or anything supernatural, but the great dread that we could not stand the fearful suffocation sufficiently to be each in our proper places and to be able to resist to the uttermost the attack which we felt must follow and so hang on at all costs to the trench we had been ordered to hold.

Courage and determination were, however, no proof against the full force of the gas and as the Canadians slowly retreated, wounded and severely gassed soldiers were abandoned to become prisoners. A new defensive line some 1,000 metres further back was established with assistance of British troops and the next day the Germans launched a series of conventional attacks near the village of St. Julien where the famous "Brooding Soldier" Canadian War Memorial now stands. After the German advance south of the village was halted, General Alderson was ordered to recapture St. Julien and "re-establish our trench line as far north as possible." This order compounded the growing chaos and led to further heavy losses. Stopping the Germans was one thing, retaking ground in a salient which was valued for reasons of Belgian pride and British prestige quite another. On 26 April yet another attack into the German positions was launched. The Lahore Division of the British Indian Army advanced until gas, used for the first time defensively, broke the impetus of the attack.

Second World War soldiers honour the fallen of the Great War. [ZK ZK 918-2]

Arthur Nantel, *9am, April 24th, 1915*. [CWM 197110261-0498]

The Canadians emerged from the battle with horrendous casualties, over 6,000 men including 1,410 who became prisoners of war. This casualty rate, 37 percent of the troops engaged, would never be exceeded, not even at the Somme. The British and Canadian press lauded the Canadian achievement and the enemy acknowledged their "tenacious determination," but behind the scenes there were serious conflicts over the conduct of the battle including sharp criticism of Brigadiers Arthur Currie and R.E.W. Turner. Many Canadian officers were equally unhappy with the performance of senior British officers. After April 1915, this tension between British and Canadian officers helped to ensure that the First Division became the core of Canada's national army rather than an "Imperial" formation drawn from a Dominion.

News of the gas attack and the valour of the country's soldiers reached Canada on 24 April before the battle was over. The newspapers reported that Canadian "gallantry and determination" had saved the situation but hinted at heavy losses. The Toronto news described the mood:

Sunday was one of the most anxious days ever experienced in Toronto, and the arrival of the officer's casualty list only served to increase the feeling that a long list including all ranks was inevitable. Crowds scanned the newspaper bulletin boards from the time of arrival of the first lists shortly before noon, until midnight, while hundreds sought information by telephone.

Historian Ian Miller, in his book *Our Glory and Our Grief*, describes the dawning awareness that whole battalions had been devastated. At first it was impossible to believe that battalions such as the 15th, made up of men from Toronto's 48th Highlanders, had been wiped out and the press assumed that many were prisoners of war. When full lists were available in early May, the truth was apparent: "half the infantry at the front have been put out of action." The events of the spring of 1915 transformed the war from a great adventure to a great crusade. A

week after the enemy introduced the horrors of gas warfare, the *Lusitania* was torpedoed off the coast of Ireland with the loss of 1,369 civilians including 150 children. Newspapers across Canada published heart-rending stories about the victims and survivors of the sinking alongside further accounts of the fighting in the Ypres Salient.

Revisionist accounts of the Great War have sought to minimize German war crimes in 1914-1915, but at the time Canada's people recognized policies designed to inspire terror for what they were. This was particularly true after the first gas attack when, to cite just one example, a letter from the front printed in the *Toronto World* informed readers that:

> … the dead are piled in heaps and groans of the wounded and dying never leave me. Every night we have to clear the roads of dead in order to get our wagons through. On our way back to base we pick up loads of wounded soldiers and bring them back to the dressing stations.

The censors could do little to prevent the publication of such letters and they proved equally unable to control the content of articles on the war. One attempt to stop the publication of Robert W. Service's gritty descriptions of his experiences as an ambulance driver was ignored by editors determined to print front line reports from the popular author and poet. Service's description of the "Red Harvest" of the trenches with its images of "poor hopeless cripples" and a man who seemed to be "just one big wound" left no room for doubt about the ugliness of war.

Festubert and Givenchy

The reverse suffered by Second British Army at Ypres did not lead to any change in British plans to support a new French offensive intended to secure Vimy Ridge. The British contribution was an attack on Aubers Ridge disguised to draw reserves away from Vimy. Despite evidence that the Germans had greatly strengthened their defences, the attack began on 9 May and quickly turned into a costly disaster. As J.P. Harris writes, "defeat was swift, bloody and complete." A second attempt later the same day was an "unmitigated disaster" with losses of 10,000 men of whom one in four died.

The failure at Aubers Ridge did not end demands for continued action on the British front. Sir Douglas Haig decided to leave the ridge to the enemy and try his luck further south at Festubert. His new plan called for a pincer movement to be preceded by a lengthy bombardment rather than the "Hurricane," a forty minute barrage, used at Aubers Ridge. For the first time, a prepared attack was to begin at night. The cost of the action, which gained modest and meaningless ground, was between 12,000 and 16,000 casualties.

The Canadians, who had lost close to one third of the 18,000 men in the division at Ypres, had been partially reinforced from the reserve battalion brought to England with the First Contingent. Despite the best efforts of officers and NCOs, two weeks was not enough time to integrate these soldiers into the rifle companies. One may reasonably ask why Third Canadian

James Mowat, *Stretcher Bearers.*
[CWM 19710261-0439]

Brigade, which had borne the brunt of the battle in the salient, was placed under command of 7th British Division and pressed into battle on 18 May? There is no good answer to this question other than the condition of 7th Division and Haig's determination to continue a pointless battle.

Sent over the top within hours of relieving the British troops, the 14th and 16th battalions made scant progress before digging in. The rest of the division arrived the next day and, despite Alderson's plea for time to study the situation before committing his troops, Haig insisted on immediate action. Two days of intense close combat for what would be called the Canadian Orchard ensued. The price: 2,468 casualties.

Coming so soon after the struggle in the salient, Festubert was a shock to many Canadians. Brigadier Arthur Currie complained bitterly about the lack of preparation and inadequate support while Sam Hughes wrote a scathing attack on Alderson which he sent to Prime Minister Borden and Lord Kitchener. As always, Hughes went off the deep end but his criticisms should not be entirely ignored. The fruitless attacks at Festubert which Hughes described as "attempting to gain a few yards…with

Gen. Alderson. [PA 1681033]

no preconceived plan of an effective drive to smash the enemy" are an accurate picture of the engagements that cost First British Army a further 16,000 casualties.

Haig took a very different view of Festubert insisting that a new attempt to break through the German defences and exploit into open country would succeed if a longer preliminary bombardment was employed. Thus the battle for Givenchy began with 211 guns firing for 48 hours before two British divisions attacked in the early evening of 15 June. Haig and Rawlinson, the Corps commander responsible for the action, were in sharp disagreement over the purpose and scope of the operation. Rawlinson continued to argue for a measured "bite and hold" approach while Haig insisted on yet another attempt to break through and exploit. Givenchy quickly turned into another costly disaster for British troops. The First Canadian Brigade under Brigadier Malcolm Mercer played a supporting role, protecting 7th

British Division's flank. Neither the British division nor the Canadian Brigade made any significant progress and the operation was called off on 18 June.

Overall, Allied losses in May and June totalled more than 200,000 men, numbers that ought to have clearly demonstrated that battles could not be won with the weapons and tactics used in 1915. The British and French field commanders were convinced that with more and better shells for the artillery, including ones filled with gas, they would break the German defences. Lord Kitchener, who was striving to create a 'New Army' which would place fifty divisions in the field, was less sure. He was preparing for a long war but admitted he had no idea how it might be won. It is evident that the British generals, like their French and German counterparts, were totally surprised by the harsh realities of trench warfare. They simply had no idea of how to get men across the zones of machine gun, mortar and artillery fire to close with the enemy. They were equally unprepared to exploit any breach in their opponents' defensive position if it should happen to occur.

Senior British officers, with a few outstanding exceptions, demonstrated a profound lack of imagination and initiative in the early years of the war. The first suggestions for a tracked armoured vehicle which could overcome barbed wire and cross trenches were made in Britain during the fall of 1914 but the army was not interested. Instead experiments were carried out by a "landships committee" formed by Winston Churchill, through his control of naval expenditures. The first such vehicles, known for security reasons as "tanks," were ready for use in

"Impregnable" Position Carried by the British

July 1916 though another year passed before large numbers were available. Steel helmets, which saved many lives, were issued by the French in early 1915 but British and Canadian troops waited another year before helmets became standard issue. The Germans made early use of trench mortars but it took eleven months to authorize the mass production of the British-invented Stokes mortar. The public was not aware of these problems but they were told of the shortage of Allied machine guns which was said to account for German success in trench warfare.

The machine gun movement, which became a popular crusade in Britain, was launched in Canada by John C. Eaton of the department store family who donated $100,000 to purchase armoured cars equipped with Colt machine guns. The concept of motorized armoured machine gun carriers was an initiative of Raymond Brutinel, a former French officer and immigrant to Canada, who organized "the first motorized armoured unit formed by any country during the war." Brutinel's First Canadian Motor Machine Gun Brigade was reinforced by the batteries created in Canada, though the static conditions on the Western Front provided little opportunity for mobile warfare and before 1918 the Brigade was used primarily in a fire support role.

During the second half of 1915 and the early months of 1916, no Canadian formation was committed to a major battle. The Second Division, raised in the

Brutinel's Motor Machine Gun Brigade.

fall of 1914, arrived in France in September 1915 and went through an extensive training process including time in the trenches. Major-General Sam Steele, an authentic western Canadian hero, commanded the division during training but Sir John French and Lord Kitchener insisted on an experienced commander offering "any British officer on the unemployed list" for the job. Sam Hughes and Prime Minister Robert Borden, determined to see Canadians in command posts, approved a compromise. A Canadian Corps under Alderson was established and two Canadian Brigadiers, Richard Turner and Arthur Currie, became divisional commanders. Steele was to take charge of Canadian troops in England.

After the series of costly and frustrating battles in the first half of 1915, the British High Command hoped to postpone participation in a major offensive until more high explosive shells were available. German success on the Eastern Front and French demands for British assistance in yet another attempt to capture Vimy Ridge forced Kitchener to agree to a battle in the flat terrain punctuated by slag heaps immediately north of Lens.

The Battle of Loos may have had to be fought for strategic reasons but it was Haig who decided it must be a breakthrough battle aimed at Douai, Valenciennes and beyond. The use of chlorine gas would, he argued, facilitate the break in battle and by using the "utmost energy" the troops were to press on through the German positions. Infantry and cavalry reserves were available for exploitation. Haig converted an action intended to contain German reserves into one of the great disasters of the war. Some 50,000 British soldiers, almost half of whom were killed or missing, were lost at Loos. Ironically this led to the dismissal of Sir John French and the promotion of Haig. Readers interested in Haig should consult *Douglas Haig: War Diaries and Letters*. The introduction provides a defence of Haig. J.P. Harris has written the most balanced account of his role in *Douglas Haig and the First World War*.

A Canadian diversion, artillery fire and a simulated gas attack, carried out by Second Division occupied the Germans opposite at a cost of 100 Canadian casualties. The men of the Second Division had at least witnessed the reality of combat on the Western Front.

The Canadians were out of the line in December when the Germans conducted an experiment with a new gas. The attack at Messines began with the release of chlorine and an intense shrapnel bombardment. The enemy then fired artillery shells containing phosgene hoping to create panic among the defenders whose gas masks could not cope with high concentrations of the new gas. Despite heavy casualties, including 120 who died from inhaling phosgene, the British held.

During the last weeks of 1915, both adversaries developed plans for operations in 1916. At the Chantilly Conference held on 6 December 1915 a vague agreement to launch coordinated offensives on the Russian, Italian and Western fronts was reached with March 1916 as the preferred date. The German commander Von Falkenhayn pre-empted these plans with his decision to "bleed the French Army white" by waging an attritional battle at Verdun beginning in February. The best overview of the role of the French Army at Verdun and elsewhere is Robert Doughty's *Pyrrhic Victory.*

Ypres remained a focus of German bombardment for the duration of the war. Here, the city centre and Cloth Hall lie in ruin. [NAS 74545854]

St. Eloi - 2-16 April 1916

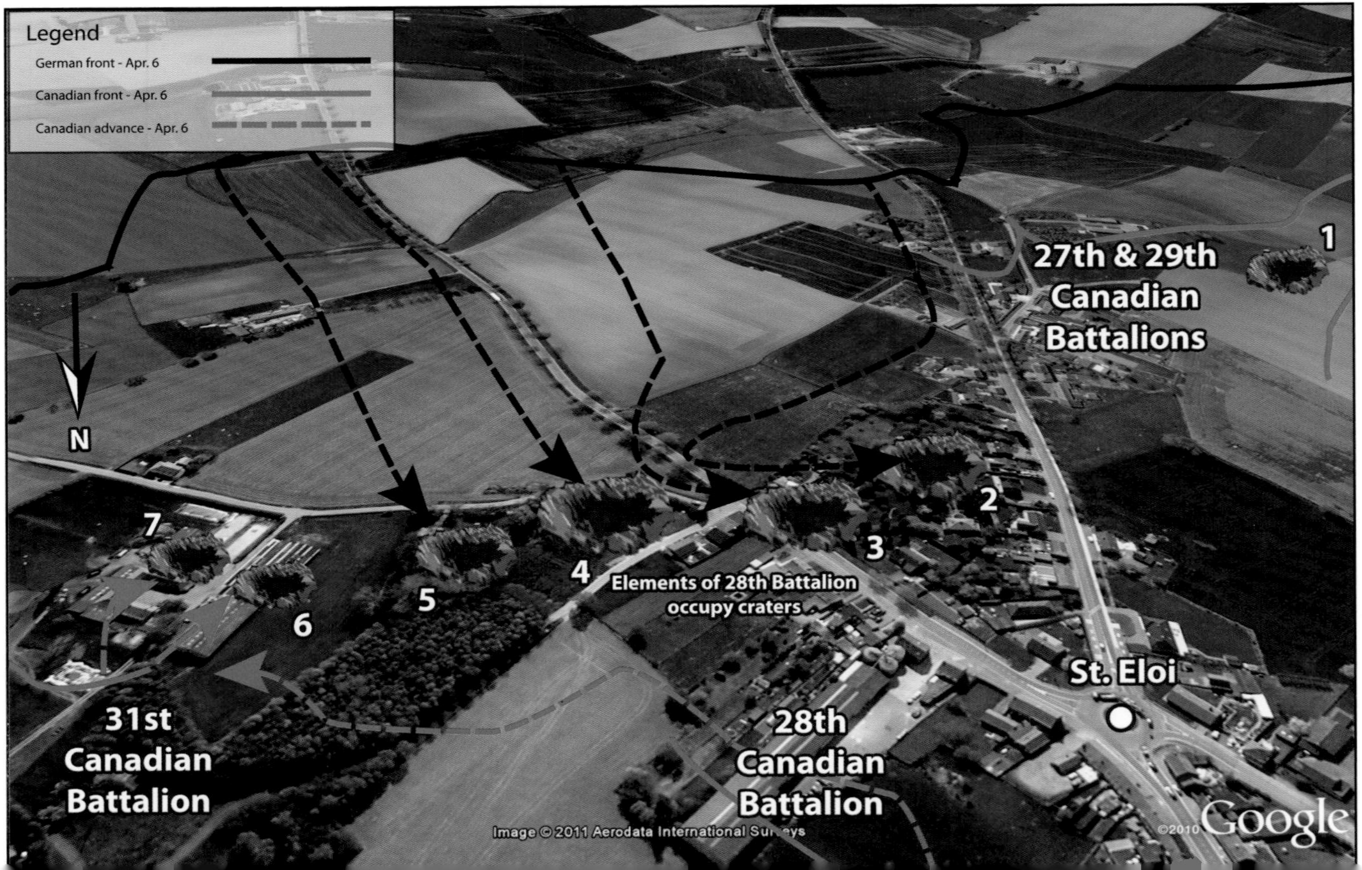

Legend
German front - Apr. 6
Canadian front - Apr. 6
Canadian advance - Apr. 6

1

27th & 29th Canadian Battalions

St. Eloi

2

3

Elements of 28th Battalion occupy craters

28th Canadian Battalion

4

5

6

7

31st Canadian Battalion

N

Image © 2011 Aerodata International Surveys

Google

St. Eloi Craters 1916

A series of small-scale diversionary attacks were ordered for the other sectors and on 14 February the German forces in the Ypres sector began an assault which captured a key position known as the "Bluff." General Plumer, commanding the Second British Army, decided to commit substantial forces to recover the Bluff and to hit back at the enemy by capturing the feature known as the "Mound" at St. Eloi, an artificial earth pile that overlooked the British positions. The St. Eloi sector had been the scene of numerous mine explosions and a British tunnelling company had completed work on six shafts that reached under the German trenches. The Third British Division was ordered to attack as soon as the mines under the enemy were exploded. Nothing worked as planned. The Mound was practically destroyed and the new craters added to the complexity of the ground in no-man's-land. And then the rains began.

Aerial reconnaissance photo of the St. Eloi craters.

The Canadian Corps was scheduled to relieve 5th British Corps after the battle but despite protests from Major-General Turner, who crawled through mud to survey the situation, Alderson obeyed Plumer's order to carry out a relief in the midst of a chaotic battle. During the relief the Germans counterattacked after an hour-long bombardment capturing the large craters numbered 2, 3, 4, and 5. The best account of the struggle in the "open grave" of St. Eloi is to be found in Tim Cook's book *At the Sharp End*. His chapters "The Murder Hole" and "Defeat and Scapegoats" offer a graphic description of life and death and a balanced account of the post-battle search for someone to blame for this ugly catastrophe and the 1,300 Canadian casualties.

The battle of St. Eloi led to another crisis in command relationships when Alderson, the Corps commander, sought to dismiss General Turner and one of his brigadiers for alleged incompetence. The new British Commander-in-Chief, General Sir Douglas Haig, refused to confirm the decision because of "the danger of a serious feud between the Canadians and the British...and because in the circumstances of the battle for the craters mistakes are to be expected." Canadian historians have tended to side with Alderson and condemn Turner, noting that political interference from Hughes and his representative Sir Max Aitken (later

One of the seven major craters at St. Eloi. [PA 4394]

Lord Beaverbrook), saved Turner and cost Alderson his job as Corps commander. But the case against Turner is made on Clausewitzian grounds suggesting that a competent commander is by definition one who reacts properly and masters the situation. If this standard is applied uniformly few generals on either side make the grade, and we are left with fallible, stubborn, imperfect humans, unable to foresee the future and almost always overwhelmed by the chaos of battle.

The Canadians, now including the Third Division, spent the summer of 1916 in familiar positions in Flanders. The enemy was still able to shell the salient from several directions making life in the forward lines both miserable and very dangerous. Many Canadian (and British) officers expressed their bitter opposition to orders to hold and attempt to expand the Ypres Salient. Sam Hughes, always suspicious of decisions made by professional British soldiers, created a major controversy when he publicly denounced the policy. By the spring of 1916 he had little credibility left and Borden moved to dismiss his troublesome minister. The men serving in the front lines knew little of these policy matters which seemed remote from the soldiers' experience of war.

Artillery fire at night. [Ernest Brooks, NAS (351) C.728]

Mount Sorrel - 2-14 June 1916

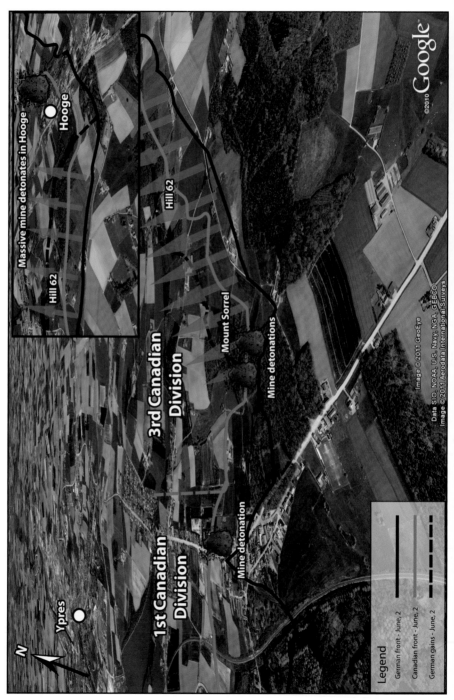

Ypres

Massive mine detonates in Hooge

Hooge

Hill 62

Hill 62

3rd Canadian Division

Mount Sorrel

Mine detonations

1st Canadian Division

Mine detonation

Legend

German front - June, 2

Canadian front - June, 2

German gains - June, 2

Image © 2011 GeoEye

Data SIO, NOAA, U.S. Navy, NGA, GEBCO

Image © 2011 Aerodata International Surveys

©2010 Google

Mount Sorrel 1916

The fallout from St. Eloi which cost Alderson command of the Corps had no impact on Plumer who had orchestrated the disaster. He continued to command Second Army. The new Canadian Corps commander was Sir Julian Byng, a veteran of the South African war who had commanded the Cavalry Corps in France before earning good reports for his leadership in supervising the withdrawal of forces from Suvla Bay in Gallipoli. Byng was to acquire a considerable reputation as the Canadian Corps commander but in 1916 he had less than three months experience leading a Corps on a quiet sector of the front.

Byng was the grandson of a Field Marshal and a prominent member of the English aristocracy. Like many other British officers, he retained his schoolboy nickname, "Bungo." His self-confidence and easy manner won him friends throughout the army and especially within the Canadian Corps. Historians have repeatedly lavished praise on Byng. Tim Cook argues "he was the single most important figure in transforming the Canadian Corps into a battle-hardened formation." Perhaps so, but in early June 1916 the problems confronting Canadian and British troops in the Ypres Salient could not be fixed by a Corps commander, however charismatic.

The Canadian Memorial at Hill 62. [Nick Lachance]

HISTORY

37

When Byng took over, the Canadian Corps was responsible for the sector of the Ypres Salient from the Menin Road to south of St. Eloi. The recently formed Third Division commanded by Major-General Malcolm Mercer held the left of the line clinging to the only part of the Ypres ridge still in Allied hands, "a flat knoll called Mount Sorrel and two slightly higher twin eminences, 'Hill 61' and 'Hill 62,' the latter known as Tor Top." From Tor Top a "broad span of largely farm land, aptly named Observatory Ridge, thrust

Corps commander Byng. [PA 1356]

nearly a thousand yards due west between Armagh Wood and Sanctuary Wood."

Despite the tactical importance of the ridge-top positions, Second Army failed to respond to growing signs that a German attack was imminent. The Canadians who took over the sector were just beginning to make changes when the attack

Mary Riter Hamilton, *Sanctuary Wood*. [LAC 1988-180-21]

struck. Two German divisions of the Wurttemburg Corps, employing the heaviest bombardment yet used in the area, overwhelmed the Canadian positions. Both General Mercer and Brigadier-General Williams, commander of the 8th Brigade, were killed early in the battle and this no doubt added to the confusion. The Germans, who had planned a bite and hold operation, quickly dug in overlooking Ypres.

Byng, who had been with the Corps less than a week, ordered an immediate counterattack that proved to be a costly failure. He then stepped back and organized an intensive artillery-based attack employing two composite brigades of First Division. The original line was restored on 13 June. The two weeks of close combat, including the loss of Hooge, a village on the Menin Road, cost the Corps close to 9,000 casualties.

German dead shown after Canadians recaptured ground lost during the Battle of Mount Sorrel, Belgium, 1916. [H.E. Knobel, PA 000186]

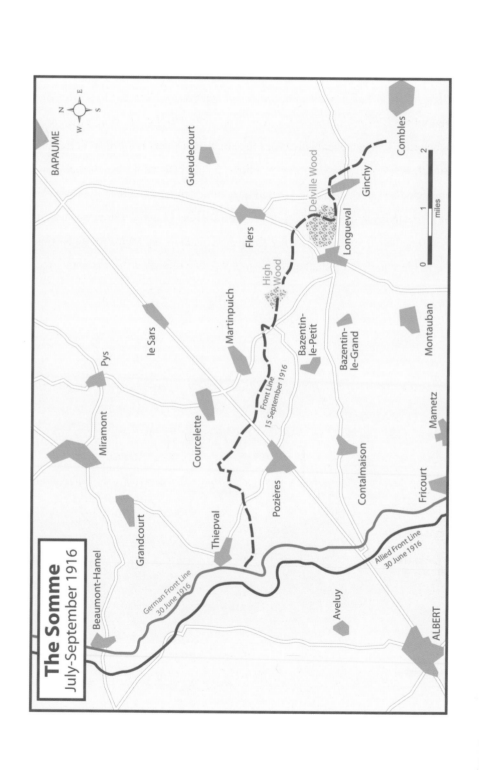

The Somme
July–September 1916

BAPAUME

Gueudecourt

Delville Wood

Combles

Ginchy

Flers

Longueval

High
Wood

Martinpuich

Bazentin-
le-Petit

Bazentin-
le-Grand

le Sars

Montauban

Pys

Front Line
15 September 1916

Miramont

Courcelette

Mametz

Contalmaison

Fricourt

Thiepval

Pozières

Grandcourt

Beaumont-Hamel

German Front Line
30 June 1916

Allied Front Line
30 June 1916

Aveluy

ALBERT

N
W   E
S

0   1   2
miles

The Somme

While the Canadians endured life and death in the Ypres Salient, German Chief of Staff Erich von Falkenhayn began the battle of Verdun. This offensive, he told the Kaiser, might win the war, especially if combined with unrestricted submarine war against all merchant shipping. Falkenhayn hoped to "bleed the French Army white" by seizing positions the French would be determined to counterattack at great cost. The battle — the longest of the war — that began on 21 February 1916, was still raging when Russia launched its most successful operation, the "Brusilov Offensive" on 4 June. The Germans who had begun accumulating reserves to meet the projected Allied offensive in the Somme were forced to transfer fifteen divisions to the east, ending any possibility of continuing offensive operations at Verdun.

The Somme offensive is now chiefly remembered for the disastrous first day, 1 July 1916 when 21,000 British soldiers were killed and 35,000 wounded, but the battle continued with pauses for re-organization for four and a half months. The political and military leaders of France and Britain had selected the Somme valley as the logical site for a major offensive because it was the only place where the armies of the two nations could fight side-by-side. Unfortunately, there was nothing else to recommend in an area of rolling chalk hills that the enemy had

Aerial view of the Somme battlefield in July taken from a British balloon near Bécourt.

Beaumont-Hamel - 1 July 1916

Hawthorn Crater

Beaumont-Hamel

Y Ravine

Danger Tree

no-man's-land

Legend

German front line

Allied front line

Allied second line

Allied third line

Communication trench

N

Google ©2010

Image © 2011 IGN-France

fortified during 1915. The Germans created their first line of defences on the forward slopes of ridge lines. Two belts of barbed wire protected three trenches; outpost line, main position and reserve, each approximately 160 metres apart. Where possible, fortified villages like Beaumont, Hamel and Thiepval were a part of the defences. Deep dugouts served to protect troops. The German second line 3,000 metres to the rear was protected by yet more barbed wire and a series of "mini-fortresses with all round defence." A third position was under construction when the attack began.

If there was any chance of success at the Somme the attackers would have to stick to the kind of "bite and hold" tactics advocated by Sir Henry Rawlinson. His plan for Fourth Army called for "seizing points of tactical importance which will provide us with good observation and which the Germans will counterattack." The object was "to kill as many Germans as possible with the least possible loss." Haig rejected such an approach as too cautious and required Fourth Army to plan for an initial advance that would capture both the first and second German positions across a 25 kilometre front after a six day preliminary bombardment. Three cavalry divisions were available for exploitation.

The results of this optimism may be viewed at a Canadian National Historic Site, the Beaumont-Hamel Newfoundland Battlefield and Memorial. Here the 8th British Corps with three divisions under command suffered enormous losses. Their crushing defeat had little to do with the tactics adopted. As Robin Prior and Trevor

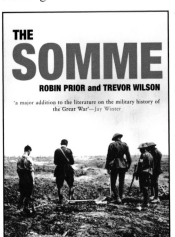

THE
SOMME
ROBIN PRIOR and TREVOR WILSON
'a major addition to the literature on the military history of the Great War'—Jay Winter

Wilson demonstrate in their indispensable book, *The Somme*, the leading brigades tried a variety of techniques where no battalion advanced in successive lines or waves. The problem was not the lack of experience of the officers and men; the catastrophe was rooted in Haig's decision to ask too much of the available artillery and in the strength of the German defences.

The Germans first position included the Y Ravine protected by the extensive barbed wire on the Hawthorn Ridge, a particularly formidable obstacle which British miners had tunnelled under and planted 18,000 kilograms of explosives.

For reasons that have never been satisfactorily explained, the Corps commander, Lieutenant-General Sir Aylmer Hunter-Weston, an officer known for arrogance and the bullying of subordinates, decided to set off the explosives ten minutes before the attack began alerting the defenders waiting on the reverse slope. The 86th and 87th Brigades of 29th Division found much of the wire uncut and the German defences largely intact. The decision to commit the reserve, 88th Brigade including the Newfoundland Regiment, to a battle that was already lost has been blamed on poor communication which led the division commander, Major-General de Lisle, to believe that one of his brigades was through the German forward defences. Both the Essex Regiment and the Newfoundlanders were subjected to intense machine gun and artillery fire and were unable to reach the German front line. "Dead men can advance no further."

The 29th Division lost 5,000 men, including 90 percent of the men of the Newfoundland Regiment (272 killed, 438 wounded), 8th Corps suffered 14,000

This photo is part of a series showing the explosion of the mine beneath Hawthorn Ridge Redoubt on 1 July 1916. [Ernest Brooks, IWM 1900-09]

A wounded man of the Newfoundland Regiment at Beaumont-Hamel. [PANL NA 6067]

casualties or about half of its rifle strength. The Newfoundland Regiment and much of the rest of the division and Corps had to be rebuilt, returning to full strength at the Somme in October. A smaller version of the famous Caribou Memorial marks the Gueudecourt battlefield where the battalion captured a major German strongpoint.

The Canadian Corps was transferred to the Somme in August and began training for the specific circumstances of the terrain. The British Army's operations had bogged down and the Canadians were to take over the sector that

Thurston Topham, *The Somme Bombardment in Full Swing.* [CWM 19710261-0725] Painted on the 29 June 1916 as an eye-witness to the impressive but ineffective bombardment. The scribbles on the side are Topham's notes from the era.

Battle of Courcelette - 15 September 1916

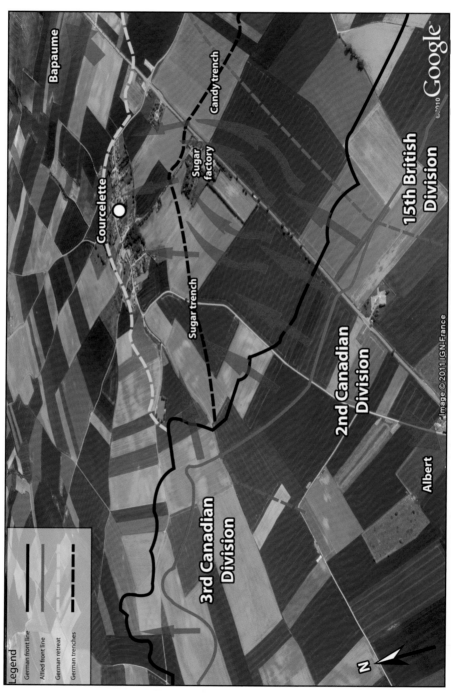

Legend
- German front line
- Allied front line
- German retreat
- German trenches

Bapaume

Candy trench

Courcelette

Sugar factory

Sugar trench

15th British Division

2nd Canadian Division

3rd Canadian Division

Albert

N

Image © 2011 IGN-France

Google ©2010

bedeviled the Australian Corps at Pozières. The Australians had suffered more than 8,000 casualties in a failed attempt to take the well-fortified Mouquet Farm. Prior and Wilson note that total casualties for the period 7 August to 12 September in the sector "cannot have been much short of 20,000." The Canadians relieved the exhausted Australians in preparation for yet another attempt to break through the German defences.

This time Haig believed a mid-September offensive would yield better results because a new weapon, the tank, would be available to support the assault divisions. Once again Haig insisted on a breakthrough plan to seize all three German positions "with a view to opening the way for the cavalry." Writing in his diary, Haig recorded his belief in the imminent collapse of German morale and the necessity of making the attack "as strong and violent as possible, and plan to go as far as possible." Haig also issued orders for a general advance by the rest of the British Army when the predicted collapse began.

The Canadian Corps joined General Hubert Gough's Reserve Army. The First Division took over the entire Corps front while Second and Third Divisions rehearsed their parts in what was to become known as the Flers-Courcelette battle. The Canadians were just one of four Corps committed to action on 15 September. Eleven divisions therefore had to share just 56 tanks. The seven allocated to the Canadians could hardly be a decisive factor.

Thurston Thopham, *A Tank in Action*. [CWM 19710261-0757]

Fortunino Matania, *The Capture of the Sugar Refinery.* [CWM 19870268-001]

The Second Canadian Division relied on a rolling barrage to take their objectives, assigning a mopping up role to the tanks. The "Sugar Factory" proved to be heavily fortified but fell to a well-rehearsed attack from three directions as the barrage lifted. Just two of the six tanks sent into action engaged the enemy. Mopping up occupied much of the morning and at 1800 hours the 5th Brigade, commanding Brigadier A. H. Macdonnell, renewed the advance with the 22nd and 25th Battalions taking Courcelette. The artillery again led the way but both battalions reported brief intense encounters. They then dealt with the inevitable counterattacks, seventeen of them over the next four days.

The division and its commander, Major-General Richard Turner, had been under a cloud since the battle of the St. Eloi craters. Courcelette, a well-managed tactical victory changed the reputation of the division. The casualty toll of 1,283 included a very high proportion, 714 killed in action but in the surreal world of the western front this was a relatively low cost victory. Unfortunately in the days that followed, casualties mounted as the Canadians were required to continue the struggle to secure the trenches beyond Courcelette.

On 26 September, First Canadian Division attempted to reach Regina Trench as part of a four division assault on Thiepval Ridge. The capture of Thiepval village and Mouquet Farm by two British divisions and limited gains by the Fourth Army allowed claims of another victory but the costs were enormous and

Wounded Canadians evacuated from Courcelette, 1916. [NAS (165) O.810]

there was no sign of a German collapse. Continuing attacks in the Somme could no longer be justified by reference to Verdun and Haig now emphasized his belief that the enemy was near the breaking point. Rain storms that turned much of the battlefield into a muddy morass did not bring an end to repeated attacks, including the final assault on Regina Trench that was secured by the 4th Canadian Division on 11 November 1916. For a detailed description of the Canadian experience, see Tim Cook's *At The Sharp End*.

The Somme cost the British 432,000 casualties – the fighting strength of twenty-five infantry divisions. French casualties added another 200,000 while the best estimate of German casualties, 500,000, includes 230,000 suffered in combat with the British. Since the British were constantly attacking, it is not surprising that they lost two men for every casualty they inflicted on the enemy.

Given the Verdun situation, a British-led offensive in the Somme valley was inevitable in 1916. The operational challenge was to fight the German Army in a cost-effective way and Haig failed to do this. Unfortunately the British Prime Minister Herbert Asquith and his successor David Lloyd George lacked the determination to control or replace Haig. Historians are sharply divided over Haig's role as Commander-in-Chief. For an overview see *Haig: A Re-Appraisal 80 Years On*.

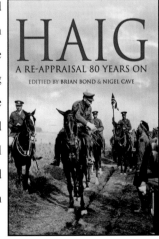

Battle of Vimy Ridge - 9 - 12 April 1917

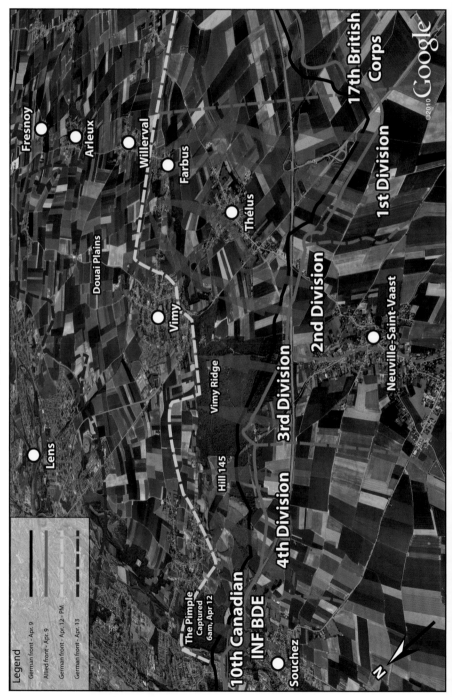

Legend

German front - Apr. 9

Allied front - Apr. 9

German front - Apr. 12 - PM

German front - Apr. 13

17th British Corps

1st Division

2nd Division

3rd Division

4th Division

10th Canadian INF BDE

Fresnoy

Arleux

Willerval

Farbus

Thélus

Douai Plains

Vimy

Vimy Ridge

Hill 145

Lens

The Pimple
Captured
6am, Apr 12

Souchez

Neuville-Saint-Vaast

N

Vimy and the Arras Offensive

Haig's policy of continuing the Somme battle after it was evident that there was little hope of defeating the enemy in 1916 was bitterly opposed by many British political leaders, including David Lloyd George who became Prime Minister in December 1916. Lloyd George's criticisms of Haig and the war of attrition on the Western Front would continue until the Armistice but in the absence of a convincing alternative strategy the British and French armies continued to plan to renew the offensive in 1917.

Lloyd George was anxious to limit the slaughter in the trenches but he was not prepared to endorse the various peace proposals put forward by the American President, Woodrow Wilson, the Pope or the German government. The peace proposals of December 1916 were widely discussed in Britain and Canada. Since it was evident that negotiations were bound to produce a settlement favourable to Germany because of its occupation of important parts of France, most of Belgium, and large areas of the Russian empire, few individuals endorsed the idea of an Armistice in 1916. As there was no hope of peace on German terms, the Kaiser and his chief advisors decided to employ "unrestricted submarine warfare" as a means of ending Britain's capacity to continue the war. This policy, implemented in February 1917, led to the United States' declaration of war against Germany on 6 April 1917.

Allied military commanders remained committed to victory on the Western Front. The British preferred a plan to try and win control of the Belgian coast but agreed to cooperate with a

American entry to the war coincided with the attack on Vimy although few Canadian leaders expected the Americans to make an immediate impact. [US Library of Congress]

French proposal for a coordinated Anglo-French attack designed to encircle and destroy large elements of the German Army. Before the "Nivelle offensive," named for the new French commander Robert Nivelle, began, the enemy withdrew to position known as the Hindeburg Line some 20 miles to the east. This manoeuvre destroyed what little prospect of success the plan had promised but the operation was not cancelled.

The British part in the April offensive, known as the Battle of Arras, included yet another attempt to capture Vimy Ridge, a feature which dominated the Lens-Douai plain to the east. The Germans did not abandon the ridge when they withdrew to the Hindenburg Line as the ground was considered of vital importance and the defences thought to be impenetrable. The Battle of Arras, like the rest of the 1917 spring offensive, yielded little beyond death and destruction, except at Vimy where the Canadian Corps, part of First British Army, won an important local victory announced to the world as "Canada's Easter gift to France." The success of the Canadian Corps has given rise to a peculiar myth which relates the capture of Vimy Ridge to the emergence of Canada as a nation. This is a theme requiring analysis of the construction of post-war memory in English-speaking Canada rather than the actual events.

Canadian historians have also been drawn to the battle for Vimy Ridge when seeking to advance the idea that the Corps was a particularly effective component of the Allied armies. The first systematic study of these issues was Bill Rawling's *Surviving Trench Warfare*, which examined the changes in weapons and tactics

William Longstaff, *Ghosts of Vimy Ridge*. [CHOC Collection, (AN O-4714)]

between 1914 and 1918. Rawling argues that "each soldier" became "a specialist with a specific role to play in battle." The Canadian Corps, he writes, "moved away from the concept of a citizen-solider who would ride and shoot to an army of technicians, which, even in infantry battalions, specialized in particular aspects of fighting battles." Rawling believes that the growing sophistication of the Canadian Corps helps to explain the dramatic success at Vimy and in the battles of 1918.

Further study of the Vimy battle should begin with the essays in *Vimy Ridge: A Canadian Reassessment*. This collection, published by WLU Press with LCMSDS Press, provides a great deal of new information based on archival research while the critical reader is able to appreciate the very different perspectives of the seventeen contributors. Gary Sheffield, a British historian, believes the Canadian Corps is best understood as a fully integrated part of the Imperial Army. For Sheffield, a firm admirer of Field Marshal Haig, the entire British Expeditionary Force, not just the Canadians, was in the process of being transformed into "a large, sophisticated, technologically advanced and highly effective army."

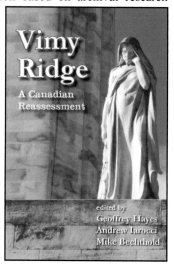

Essays by Paul Dickson, Mark Humphries, Bill Rawling, and Tim Cook explore this process, and the book provides an account of the experience of each of the Canadian divisions at Vimy. This theme is further developed by Christopher Pugsley, a historian who has studied the Anzac experience. He stresses the debt the Australians and New Zealanders owed to the Canadian Corps. Puglsey believes that the Canadians led the way in re-organizing their rifle companies so that each of the four platoons (of 28 to 44 men) would include two sections of riflemen, who would also have rifle grenades, a section of Lewis guns to provide immediate covering fire and a bombing section armed with hand grenades. Puglsey credits Byng with implementing a standard platoon-focused battle doctrine in all four divisions of the Corps in December 1916. These changes, Pugsley suggests, were then implemented across the BEF beginning in February 1917.

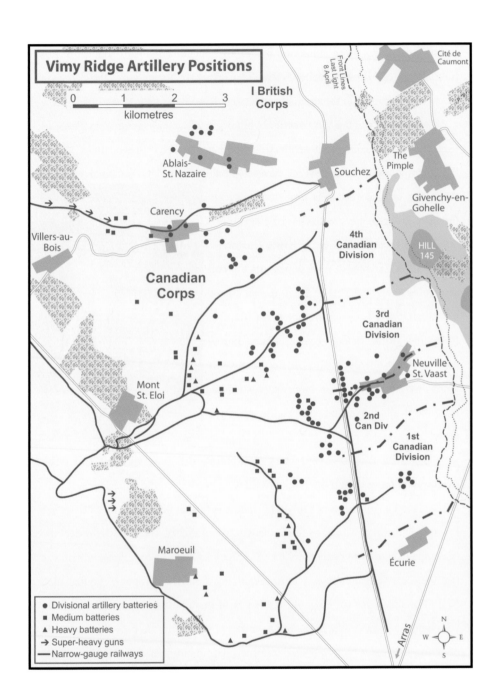

Vimy Ridge Artillery Positions

0   1   2   3
kilometres

I British Corps

Front Lines
Last Light
8 April

Cité de Caumont

Ablais-St. Nazaire

Souchez

The Pimple

Carency

Givenchy-en-Gohelle

Villers-au-Bois

4th Canadian Division

HILL 145

Canadian Corps

3rd Canadian Division

Neuville St. Vaast

Mont St. Eloi

2nd Can Div

1st Canadian Division

Maroeuil

Écurie

- Divisional artillery batteries
- Medium batteries
- ▲ Heavy batteries
- → Super-heavy guns
- — Narrow-gauge railways

Arras

N
W — E
S

Mark Humphries is less sure. He notes that the actual instructions issued by GHQ stressed the need to attack first in waves following the artillery barrage, then attacking the enemy with fixed bayonet. Platoon fire and movement tactics were reserved for situations where the normal advance was held up. None of this was particularly new, as one war diarist, quoted by Humphries, recorded "It will always be the work of the man with the rifle and bayonet to assault a position...the Lewis Gunner to resist a counterattack and support further advance, the bomber to mop up..."

There is much to be learned from these commentaries on the evolution of tactics, but Vimy was primarily a set-piece battle dominated by artillery. The troops were carefully rehearsed to move quickly to their assigned objectives relying on "one heavy gun for every 20 yards of front and a field gun for every ten yards, twice the density available at the Somme." This enormous firepower, most of it British, together with the elaborate counter-battery work of British and Canadian gunners permitted the Corps to move steadily across the sloping, featureless terrain. By early afternoon three of the four divisions had reached the crest of the ridge. When Hill 145, the objective of 4th Division, fell three days later the entire ridge was in Canadian hands. The Royal Flying Corps also played a major role in the Battle of Arras, obtaining air superiority and attacking the targets the Army requested. The cost, 275 aircraft and 421 casualties, was long remembered as "Bloody April" in the story of British airpower. The army's

Canadian troops advance at Vimy Ridge, 9 April 1917. [PA 1496]

Stretcher Bearers and POWs help the Canadian wounded at Vimy Ridge. [PA 001021]

victory had also been costly — 3,598 dead and 6,664 wounded — but the attack, Rawling argues, "ended with a different balance between costs and results."

Securing Vimy Ridge and thus protecting the left flank of Third Army's main effort, an advance to Cambrai was the major task assigned to the Canadian Corps and Henry Horne's First Army. Third Army, attacking with ten divisions plus infantry and cavalry reserves, captured all its initial objectives, the same Black, Brown and Blue lines seized by the Canadians at Vimy. Momentum was soon lost as the weather, casualties, exhaustion, and the arrival of German reserves stabilized the front a few miles beyond the start line. Both Third and First Armies demonstrated prowess at set-piece attacks, with massive amounts of artillery, but skill at breaking into the German defences did not lead to a break-through, never mind a break-out.

The capture of Vimy Ridge did not end Canadian participation in the Battle of Arras. The Nivelle offensive had been heralded as an action that could bring the war to an end but it began with heavy losses, 40,000 French casualties on the first day, and slight gains on the ground. Nivelle remained committed to the offensive and on 20 April began a determined assault on the Chemin des Dames Ridge that continued until 9 May. French losses were estimated at 187,000 men, German casualties reached a total of 168,000.

Haig would have preferred to cease operations in the Arras sector and move resources north for his cherished offensive in Flanders, but the British were

Canadians celebrate after the capture of Vimy Ridge. [PA 001353]

obliged to assist Nivelle by maintaining pressure on the Arras front. On 23 April, ten British divisions launched what is known as the Second Battle of the Scarpe. On 28 April, a second attempt to breach the German defences with six divisions including First Canadian was launched. Michael Bechthold who has studied these actions closely notes that Currie, still commanding the First Division, insisted on a two stage operation with an emphasis on planning to defeat German counterattacks. The Canadian success at Arleux was the only bright note on a day in which other divisions failed to make even limited gains.

On 3 May Haig began another attempt to reach the Drocourt-Quéant line employing fourteen divisions in the Third Battle of the Scarpe. "There were," Bechthold writes, "only two small successes...The First Anzac (Australian and New Zealand Army Corps) captured Bullecourt and First Canadian Division captured and held Fresnoy." British historian J.P. Harris writes "The capture of Fresnoy was the culminating point of a series of brilliant successes by the Canadian Corps during the Arras battles and the relieving feature of a day which many who witnessed it consider the blackest day of the war." The "blackest day," so named because of heavy casualties and growing recognition that any further attempt to break the Hindenburg Line were unlikely to succeed.

Haig was now planning to switch the main British effort to the Ypres front but he required the continuation of operations in the Arras sector to mislead the enemy. For the Canadians this meant attacking in the Souchez-Avion sector in May and the implementation of a new policy of heavy raids designed to inflict casualties but not hold ground in June. Then on 7 July, as the build-up for the Flanders offensive continued, Haig ordered First Army to increase the scale of diversionary attacks.

Byng's successful leadership of the Canadian Corps won him promotion to command of Third Army. His successor, Lieutenant-General Sir Arthur Currie, took command of the Corps on 9 June and was quickly confronted with an outline plan for a frontal assault on the coal mining centre of Lens. Currie studied the plan and came to the conclusion that the bare chalk rise north of the city, known for its height in metres as Hill 70, should be seized first and carefully defended against the inevitable German counterattacks. Only then could an attack on the city be considered. Horne and Haig agreed to Currie's proposal.

Continuous rain postponed the Hill 70 operation until 15 August when the First and Second Divisions, each with two brigades forward, attacked and captured the first and second German position on the crest of the hill. They then took sections of the Green line on the eastern reverse slope. A diversionary attack by 4th Canadian Division further disorganized the enemy who failed to appreciate the commanding view of the battlefield now in Canadian hands. Successive, poorly organized counterattacks were destroyed by observed artillery fire and machine guns. By 18 August the enemy was forced to concede the hill.

Unfortunately, Currie's orders were to push the Germans out of Lens and he proceeded to plan a second battle for 21 August. Both Second and Fourth Divisions were committed to an advance into the ruined city and both suffered significant losses before the confused affair was called off on 25 August. The Canadians suffered 4,000 casualties between 21 and 25 August but were unable to hold any of their objectives in the city. A renewed attack was ordered for September but was cancelled when the Canadians were ordered north to join the battle for Passchendaele Ridge. Andrew Godefroy has edited a collection of essays titled *Great War Command: Historical Perspectives on Canadian Army Leadership 1914-1918* that offers interesting background on Currie, Turner, and other senior Canadian commanders.

Hill 70, 1916. [CWM 19940001-435_a]

Hill 70 August,1917. [CWM 19940001-435_b]

Passchendaele - 22 October - 6 November 1917

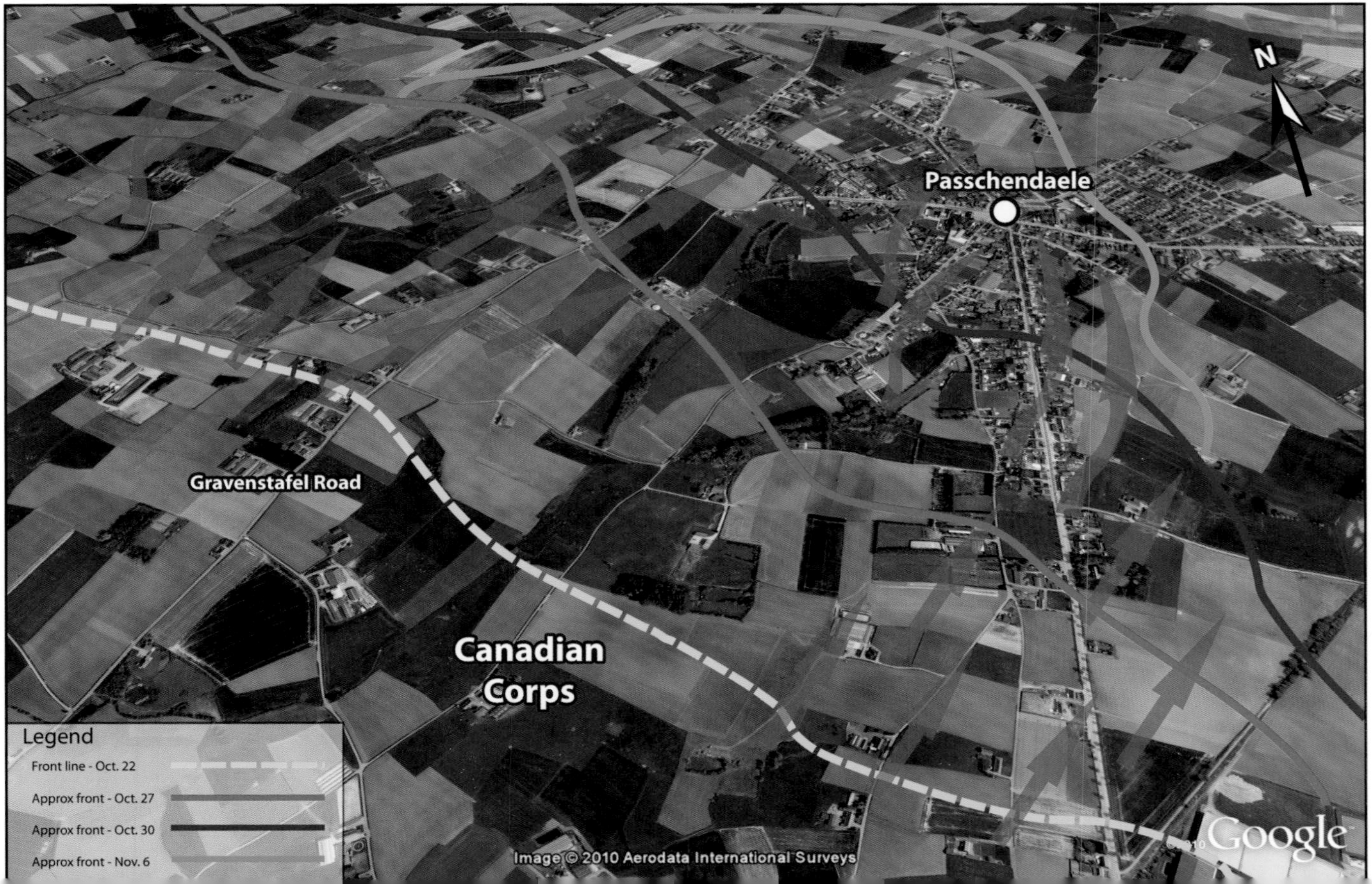

Passchendaele

Canadian Corps

Gravenstafel Road

N

Google

Image © 2010 Aerodata International Surveys

Legend

Front line - Oct. 22

Approx front - Oct. 27

Approx front - Oct. 30

Approx front - Nov. 6

Passchendaele and Cambrai 1917

By early May 1917 as the Arras offensive was winding down, British and French politicians and Generals met in Paris to plan future action. Robert Nivelle had been fired and Philippe Pétain had become Chief of the General Staff. Pétain knew there was a growing morale crisis in the French Army, though the first signs of mutiny were still a month away. He made it clear that if further offensive action was planned for 1917 it would have to be carried out by the British Army. Haig made the case for a Flanders offensive aimed at clearing the Belgian coast. The Chief of the Imperial General Staff Sir William Robertson and the politicians accepted this proposal but Robertson, long an advocate of a step by step approach declared:

> It is no longer a question of aiming at breaking through the enemy's front and aiming at distant objectives. It is now a question of wearing down and exhausting the enemy's resistance…relentlessly attacking with limited objectives and making the fullest use of our artillery. By this means we hope to gain our ends with the minimum loss possible.

No one present at the meeting addressed the contradiction between Robertson's caution and Haig's ambitious plans. His orders for a major operation on the Ypres front, with the object of securing the Belgian coast and advancing to the Dutch frontier were issued on 2 May. The outline plan called for a two-stage

Douglas Culham, *Mud Road to Passchendaele*. [CWM 19890222-001]

attack: to secure the Messines Ridge in early June, and begin the more ambitious campaign in July.

The Messines Ridge which overlooked Ypres from the south east was one of the most thoroughly defended positions on the Western Front. It was, however, subject to observed artillery fire from still higher ground and vulnerable to underground attack by tunneling companies. On 7 June 1917, nineteen mines were exploded under the ridge, destroying and demoralizing the defenders. A rapid British advance behind a barrage followed. Six hours later the entire ridge was in British hands. Operational plans called for a further advance but German reserves and especially their artillery restored the front. Messines was a significant British victory. A lessons learned approach would have again emphasized the value of limited attacks, but Haig preferred to believe that an aggressive Flanders offensive was now more certain of success. He urged a skeptical British War Cabinet to concentrate energies on the Western Front because, "Germany was within six months of total exhaustion of her available manpower if fighting continues at its present intensity." Haig reassured the politicians that he had no intention of entering into a continuous offensive with heavy losses, and no one asked how heavy losses could be avoided if fighting was to be at its current intensity.

The Germans used the lull between Messines and the main offensive to add defensive lines and strong points, including positions on Passchendaele Ridge. With nine German divisions available there was no apparent lack of manpower.

The British assault divisions trained and rehearsed as they had before the Vimy-Arras offensive and much attention was paid to the tactics to be employed by the remodelled platoons. Air superiority provided a detailed knowledge of the enemy and his gun positions, greatly assisting counter-battery planning. The bombardment began on 16 July. Two weeks later eleven divisions went over the top along an eight mile front. Hubert Gough, the Army Commander, believed a 4,000 to 5,000 yard advance was possible on the first day and planned accordingly, diluting the firepower available for the initial phase.

The first day of Third Ypres, 31 July, produced gains of up to 2,000 yards and 27,000 British casualties. The German counterattacks were defeated and the steady rain, which was to continue through most of August, hampered movement

A Canadian field gun bombarding enemy lines. The shells stacked to the left represent just a fraction of what would have been fired during a heavy bombardment. [NAS (186) X.25018]

and contributed to the failure of British attacks launched on 10, 16 and 19 August.

Haig and Gough were sharply criticized for the failure of the August battles but no one had the courage to challenge Haig's argument that "final victory might be won by December" if more manpower and guns could be found. After a lengthy pause for the ground to dry and reinforcements to be trained, nine divisions, including First Anzac Corps, mounted a major attack to gain control of the Passchendaele Ridge. An advance of 1,200 yards at a cost of 21,000 casualties ought to have brought the Flanders offensive to a close, but again Haig persisted and a further 15,000 casualties were suffered in the capture and holding of Polygon Wood.

German losses were also heavy and Haig believed "decisive results were now possible." On 4 October, twelve divisions attacked seizing deliberately limited objectives. This action, known as Broodseinde, was seen as a great Anzac success, but before other such attacks could be prepared the autumn rains began in earnest. The battlefield was transformed into a quagmire.

Despite the extraordinary conditions, further attacks were ordered. On 9 October the British and Australians suffered 15,000 casualties in a failed attempt to secure Passchendaele Ridge. If the Flanders offensive was to continue, fresh troops had to be found, and Haig decided that the Canadians who had been

Canadian Pioneers carrying trench mats with wounded and prisoners in background during the Battle of Passchendaele. [PA 3192366]

brought north to exploit success must instead fight in the sucking mud of Flanders to secure Passchendaele village.

After the battle, Currie maintained that he had tried to keep the Corps out of Flanders, but there is no contemporary evidence for this, or for stories about Haig visiting his headquarters to persuade Currie to agree. The Haig diary mentions the Canadian reluctance to serve under General Gough, but makes no suggestion of further hesitation. The Canadians arrived in Ypres two weeks before they attacked towards the ridge. Confronted with an endless expanse of water-filled shell craters and the detritus of months of a brutal conflict including unburied bodies, Currie was determined to stage a carefully controlled artillery-based battle advancing on the ridge in a series of short bounds. The first advance on 26 October was successful in that the Canadians dug in 500 yards beyond their start line. Neither the Australians on their right nor the British on the left were able to keep pace. The second phase began on 30 October and the Canadians moved onto the ridge taking the ruins of Passchendaele on 6 November. This placed them in a deeper salient subject to continuous German fire which added to the casualty toll already above 12,000 for the two week battle.

Currie and a number of historians included Passchendaele in the list of Canadian victories but there was little glory to be found in Flanders in 1917. The best account of the battle is to be found in Prior and Wilson *Passchendaele: The Untold Story*. For the Canadian experience consult Cook, *Shock Troops*.

The Canadian Corps, which had suffered more than 16,000 casualties during its brief tour in the mud of Flanders, was not involved in the battle of Cambrai, 20 November 1917, but the Canadian Cavalry Brigade and the Royal Newfoundland Regiment were in the heat of the action. The idea for a new offensive developed within Byng's Third Army which was holding the sector south of Arras, an area which had not been subjected to massive destruction. By combining predicted artillery fire with tanks to overcome barbed wire that otherwise could only be cut by extended shelling, Byng hoped to achieve surprise, pierce the Hindenburg Line and pass the cavalry through the breach to roll up the German front.

This scheme, which reflected Byng's background as a cavalry officer, was far too ambitious for the circumstances of late 1917 and after initial dramatic success, celebrated in England by ringing of church bells, the troops of Third Army found themselves in a deep salient and ill-prepared for a German counterattack.

The 29th Division, including the Royal Newfoundland Regiment, was held in reserve until the Hindenburg Line was broken; it then moved forward seizing Masnières, Nine Wood and Marcoing. The Canadian Cavalry Brigade, attached to the 5th British Cavalry Division followed up the advance and during the afternoon a squadron of the Fort Garry Horse while in the lead found a crossing of the St. Quentin Canal, captured a German gun battery, and scattered a German infantry battalion in a dramatic charge, which won a Victoria Cross for Lieutenant Harcus Strahan who lived to receive the award.

British historian Simon Robbins, in his study of British generalship on the Western Front, concludes that during the period 1915-1917, the "undue optimism of the higher command was one of the direct causes of failure." The planning process was "too ambitious with the result that in nearly every major operation in France the irrepressible optimism of the Higher Formations carried on the offensive beyond the point when...it had ceased to show a profit because they never knew when to take their profit and stop."

Blinded by optimism, Haig failed to grasp the fact that although suffering from much distress, the Germans were far from collapsing during 1916 and 1917 but were strategically on the defensive.

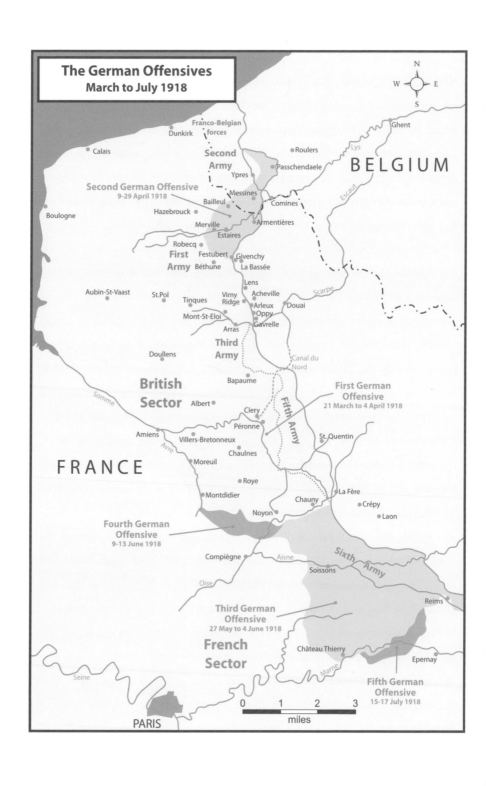

The German Offensives
March to July 1918

N
W — E
S

Franco-Belgian
forces
Dunkirk
Ghent
Calais
Roulers
Lys
Second
Army
Passchendaele
BELGIUM
Ypres
Second German Offensive
9-29 April 1918
Messines
Escaut
Bailleul
Comines
Boulogne
Hazebrouck
Armentières
Merville
Estaires
Robecq
First
Festubert
Givenchy
Army
Béthune
La Bassée
Aubin-St-Vaast
Lens
St.Pol
Vimy
Acheville
Tinques
Ridge
Arleux
Douai
Mont-St-Eloi
Oppy
Scarpe
Arras
Gavrelle
Third
Doullens
Army
Canal du
Nord
British
Bapaume
First German
Offensive
Sector
Albert
Clery
21 March to 4 April 1918
Somme
Fifth Army
Amiens
Péronne
Villers-Bretonneux
St. Quentin
Avre
Chaulnes
FRANCE
Moreuil
Roye
La Fère
Montdidier
Chauny
Crépy
Noyon
Laon
Fourth German
Offensive
9-13 June 1918
Compiègne
Aisne
Sixth
Soissons
Army
Oise
Third German
Reims
Offensive
27 May to 4 June 1918
French
Château Thierry
Sector
Epernay
Marne
Seine
Fifth German
Offensive
15-17 July 1918

0   1   2   3
miles

PARIS

The German Spring Offensive 1918

The attritional battles of 1917, which led to mutinies within the French Army, seriously weakened the British and Commonwealth forces on the Western Front. All indices of declining morale, including desertion rose significantly. Censorship reports on soldiers letters noted a lack of confidence in senior commanders and a growing belief that the war could not be won. The collapse of the Russian armies and the negotiations that ended in the Treaty of Brest-Litovsk allowed the Germans to transfer a large number of divisions from the Eastern Front, increasing the likelihood of a major German offensive in 1918. As Haig told the War Cabinet, the whole British Army is "exhausted and much reduced in strength." The only divisions "fit for duty" in the front line are "those belonging to the Australian and Canadian Corps."

The manpower situation forced the British Army to reduce the size of the each of its divisions from 12 to 9 battalions, and even then many units would remain under strength. The Canadians, Australians and New Zealanders retained the older order of battle marking the Australian and Canadian Corps as the strongest formations in the BEF.

The British War Office wanted the Canadians to organize two Corps with six of the smaller divisions but Currie argued for strengthening his powerful four-division Corps. He recommended breaking up the Canadian 5th Division in England, both to provide reinforcements and as a source for his plans to provide the Corps with additional artillery, engineers and infantry reserves sufficient to supply each battalion with one hundred extra men. Throughout 1918 the Canadian Corps was the most powerful Corps in the BEF, twice as strong as a normal British Corps of three divisions. This and other aspects of Currie's leadership are outlined in Mark Humphries (Editor), *The Selected Papers of Sir Arthur Currie.*

The Selected Papers of

Sir Arthur Currie

Diaries, Letters, and Report to the Ministry, 1917-1933

Edited by Mark Osborne Humphries

By February 1918, the British and Dominion divisions were struggling to build defences along a 123-mile front in anticipation of a major German offensive. The enemy struck on 21 March, attacking on both sides of the River Somme against the Third and Fifth British Armies. The Germans had seventy-eight divisions available for the spring of 1918 with specially selected storm trooper formations to lead Operation Michael, the first of three major operations, was initially successful especially against Fifth Army in the sector south of the Somme. Brigadier Raymond Brutinel's First Canadian Motor Machine Gun Brigade was dispatched south to assist Fifth Army and during the retreat towards Amiens, forty armoured cars saw action for nineteen consecutive days. Seventy-five percent of the brigade's combat troops became casualties, but they played a significant role in slowing the German advance.

The Canadian Cavalry Brigade was also committed in the Amiens front providing a dismounted force of 800 men to help defend the Crozat Canal and assist the withdrawal of British forces in the area. The Canadian brigade's moment of glory came on 29 March when the Royal Canadian Dragoons, Fort Garry Horse and Lord Strathcona's Horse fought the battle of Moreuil Wood in defence of Amiens.

On 28 March, the Germans launched their second operation code-named Mars at the boundary between First and Third Armies. The Second Canadian Division

Alexander Young, *Cite Jeanne D'arc; Hill 70 in the Distance*. [CWM 19710261-018]

had come under command of Third Army on 27 March as did First Division the following day. Second Division was involved in Third Army's defensive battle south of Arras, repelling local attacks and staging raids on the Germans. The division did not return to the Canadian Corps until 1 July.

Currie also lost control of his other two divisions leading him to protest that this was tactically unsound as well as contrary to Canadian government policy. Currie carried his protests to England where Sir Edward Kemp, the Canadian Cabinet Minister for Overseas Services, pressured the British Government to meet Currie's wishes. There are several biographies of Currie of which the best is by A.S.M. Hyatt. Tim Cook's, *The Madmen and the Butcher* is also recommended. *The Selected Papers of Sir Arthur Currie,* edited by Mark Humphries, offers an opportunity to get to know Currie through his letters and diary.

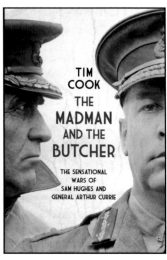

Haig was to complain that "some people in Canada regard themselves as 'allies' rather than fellow citizens in the Empire" and he contrasted the cooperative attitude of the Anzacs with the attitude of the Canadians. The consequence of all of this was the restoration of the Canadians Corps and the limitation of its role during the spring offensive to the defence of the Vimy-Lens area.

"Georgette," the German offensive in Flanders, began on 9 April and forced the British to abandon Passchendaele Ridge and retire from Armentières. With thirty-one divisions available, the German Fourth Army appeared to be overwhelming the thirteen British and French divisions in the sector and Haig issued his famous "backs to the wall" order. Fortunately, Flanders mud, logistics and the determination of the defenders stopped the German advance at the edge of Ypres.

The German's had not achieved a breakthrough and had suffered terrible losses but so had the British. The German decision to focus the next attack on the French Army at the Chemin des Dames made little sense. The offensive, code-

Battle of Amiens - 8-11 August 1918

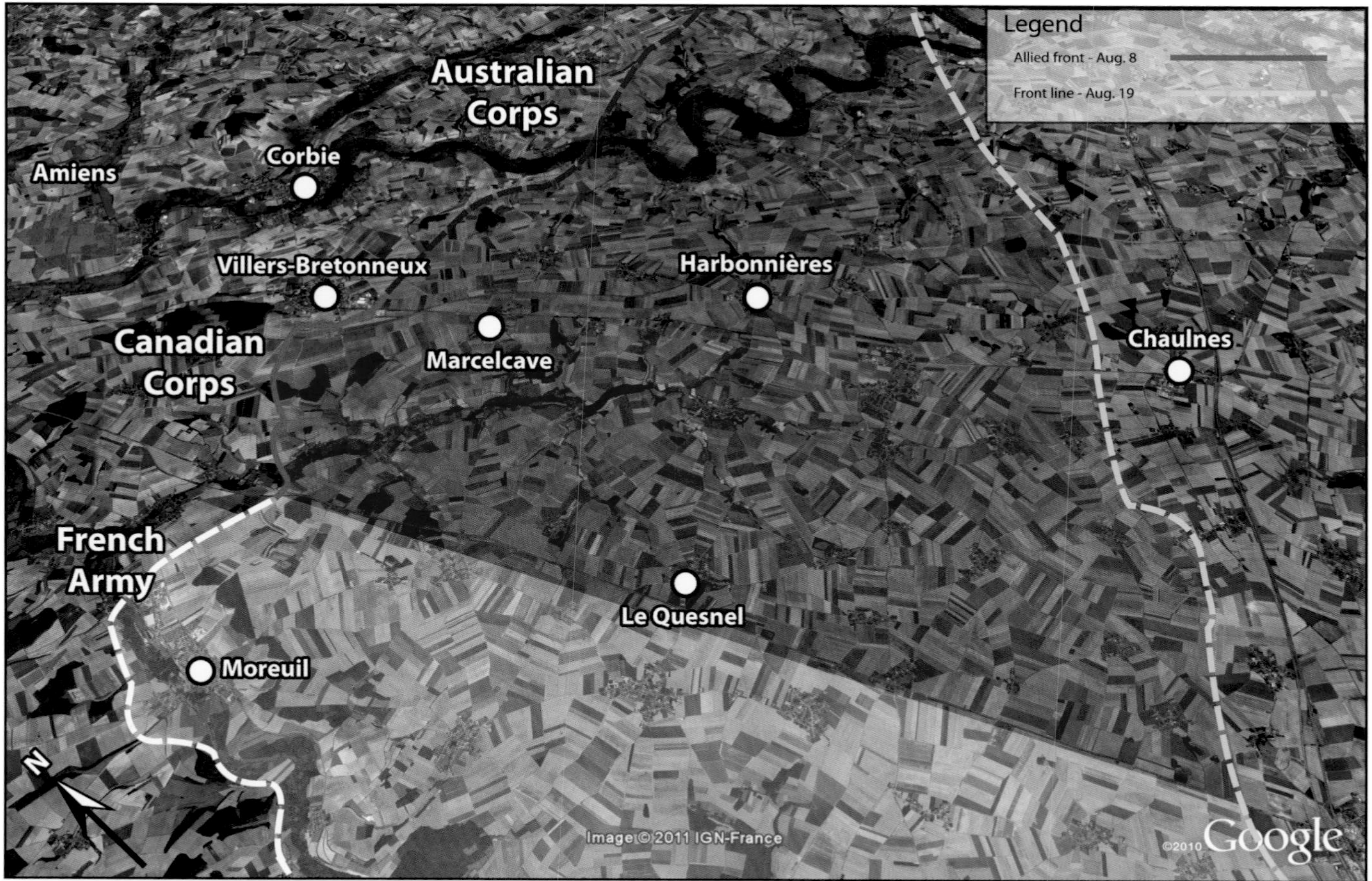

Legend
Allied front - Aug. 8
Front line - Aug. 19

Chaulnes

Harbonnières

Le Quesnel

Australian Corps

Corbie

Amiens

Villers-Bretonneux

Marcelcave

Canadian Corps

French Army

Moreuil

Google ©2010

Image ©2011 IGN-France

N

named "Blucher," began on 27 May and continued until 18 July when the French Army mounted the great counter-offensive known as the Second Battle of the Marne, the action that spelled the end of German ambitions to win the war in the west.

The German offensives of 1918 were a gamble that failed. By the beginning of August the German Army had suffered close to one million casualties and needed to defend an additional 100 kilometres of front line. Worse, they had traded their carefully fortified defensive zone for hastily prepared positions with little depth. Morale problems and the rapid spread of influenza, which affected the German Army before the virus reached the Allied armies, further weakened the Kaiser's forces.

The Battle of Amiens

Allied leaders began to prepare a major counter-offensive in the Somme valley, but the operational plan was influenced by the Australian success at Le Hamel village east of Amiens. General Sir John Monash, the aggressive Australian Corps commander, had attacked without any preliminary bombardment using forty tanks to support his infantry division (with an American battalion) to capture the position in just 40 minutes.

German and Austrian POWs following the Battle of Amiens. [GDHI]

Le Hamel served as a model for Rawlinson, the commander of Fourth Army, who planned the Amiens offensive. Rawlinson was determined to achieve surprise but he demanded the transfer of the Canadians to his army so that the two strongest Corps in the BEF could lead the attack. All four Canadian divisions were brought south in secrecy during the first days of August, a triumph of staff work.

The main battle was fought on the Plaine du Santerre, an area of "vast fields of wheat, barley and oats interspersed with orchards and brick-walled villages... ideal ground...for tank and infantry co-operation." North of the Somme British Third Corps faced much more complex terrain with a succession of ridges to be overcome. The 31st Corps (French First Army) was to advance in step with the Canadians protecting their right flank. Brutinel's "Independent Force," composed of two Motor Machine Gun Brigades, maintained contact with the French using its mobility to great advantage.

Maj. Gen. F.F. Worthington taking the salute at Camp Borden in 1956, in the armored car he used in the First World War as a Lieutenant with Brutinel's Motor Machine Gun Brigade. Alongside him is Maj. Gen. S.F. Clark, head of Central Command.

The battle was an army-level operation and could only succeed through co-operation especially between the Australians and Canadians. Allied intelligence reports described the ten German divisions in the battle zone as weak and thinly spread. For once, intelligence proved accurate. Amiens is often remembered as a tank battle as Fourth Army's order of battle included 324 of the new Mark V and

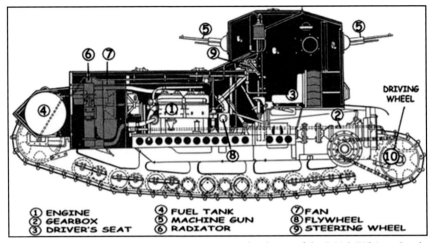

① ENGINE   ④ FUEL TANK   ⑦ FAN
② GEARBOX   ⑤ MACHINE GUN   ⑧ FLYWHEEL
③ DRIVER'S SEAT   ⑥ RADIATOR   ⑨ STEERING WHEEL

DRIVING WHEEL

The design of the British "Whippet" tank.

96 Mark A "Whippet" tanks. Each Canadian division was allotted a battalion of 36 heavy tanks plus six Mark IV supply tanks. Additional supply tanks were made available to support the engineers.

As with all battles on the Western Front, the artillery played a principal role. Over 2,000 guns supported the attack, 646 for the 8.5 kilometre front attacked by the Canadians. The attempt to achieve surprise meant no preliminary bombardment and no opportunity to register guns for counter-battery. At 0420 hours on 8 August the Australians and Canadians moved forward against a startled enemy beaten down by a hurricane of high explosive. Early morning mist helped to add tactical to operational surprise.

The Second Canadian Division's first major obstacle was the fortified village of Marcelcave. The 4th Brigade, which was to lead the attack, had been under artillery fire for more than an hour when the Allied barrage began. The 28 Mark V tanks available assisted the infantry advance but Marcelcave could only be entered after "a punishing forty-five minute artillery bombardment reduced much of the village to rubble." The remaining German soldiers forced the Canadians into a battle for the ruins before the advance could continue. Good co-operation between 7th Australian Brigade and the Canadians assisted both brigades in the rapid penetration of the "Green Line" which was secure by 0745, less than four hours after the advance began. The 5th Brigade then took over the Canadian advance, reaching the "Red Line" by early afternoon. Major-General Henry

Burstall committed 6th Brigade to the final phase, the occupation of the "Blue Line" which was won before dark.

The Victoria Cross.

In the centre, First Canadian Division had run into strong resistance at Hangard Woods where enemy machine guns, well protected by barbed wire, required extraordinary efforts by small groups of men. Two Victoria Crosses were awarded in this action, Private John Croak and Corporal H. Good both of the 13th (Black Watch) Battalion. Once through the crust, First Division reached the "Blue Line" by early evening.

Major-General L.J. Lipsett's Third Division faced the most challenging tasks. The lead brigade was to advance along the main Amiens-Roye road which was naturally well defended. The French Corps on their right flank employed an hour-long artillery barrage before attacking and this obviously could not begin until the Canadian advance was underway. Fortunately, Brutinel's force acted swiftly, protecting the exposed flank. The division's left flank straddled the River Luce which was bordered by marshes, making much of it impassable. This terrain feature forced Lipsett to employ two brigades with 9th Brigade committed to an exceptionally narrow front south of the river. Their first task: cleaning "Rifle" or "Dodo" Woods.

The 43rd Battalion (Cameron Highlanders) and the 94th French Infantry Regiment co-operated closely in this action creating an international company composed of a platoon from each army to assist the attack. Canadian engineers played a crucial role in maintaining momentum, repairing bridges and building pontooned cork footbridges across the marshy Luce valley.

North of the river, Third Division's 8th Brigade cleared Hangard Woods and captured the village. The 7th Brigade, in reserve, advanced along the main road behind a new barrage designed to bring them to the Red Line. Despite gas shells and cratered ground they reached their objective, dug in and watched in amazement as the Third Cavalry Division with the Canadian Brigade in the lead came forward to test the long-defended chances of a breakout. The "Whippet" tanks, in support, proved too slow for the cavalry and German machine guns cut down horses and riders. The Canadian brigade lost 245 men in a series of "gallant but futile charges." Elsewhere, the cavalry enjoyed some success, one regiment intercepting a trainload of reinforcements and taking 600 prisoners.

Haig and Rawlinson believed that the Amiens-Roye road was the best axis of advance and Currie had placed the 4th Canadian Division in position to exploit whatever success his infantry and the Third Calvary Division had obtained. The Germans were equally committed to defending the sector and despite the commitment of fresh troops the enemy held a key Canadian objective, Le Quesnel, (where the Canadian Memorial for the Amiens battle is located) against repeated attacks. Le Quesnel fell the next morning, but the strength of the German defence pointed to a significant change in the rhythm of the battle. The Canadians had advanced 13 kilometres, a distance unprecedented on the Western Front but there was no breakthrough. Despite a further advance of up to 3 kilometres on 9 August it was becoming evident that German reinforcements, nine additional divisions by 10 August, were closing off the chances of reaching Péronne or Roye. Just 38 tanks were available across the entire Fourth Army front and the Allied soldiers were exhausted. Currie and other commanders sought to persuade Haig to call off the offensive initially. Currie was not just a highly successful commander; he was also the head of Canada's national army. His written protest persuaded Haig to end the Amiens offensive. Sir Julian Byng's Third Army was to stage the next attack while the Canadians returned to First Army and the Arras sector to prepare for a major assault on the Hindenberg Line. You may wish to read J.P Harris, *Amiens to the Armistice* for background on the overall campaign, and Shane Schreiber, *Shock Army of the British Empire*, for the Canadian story.

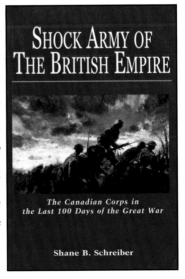

SHOCK ARMY OF
THE BRITISH EMPIRE

*The Canadian Corps in
the Last 100 Days of the Great War*

Shane B. Schreiber

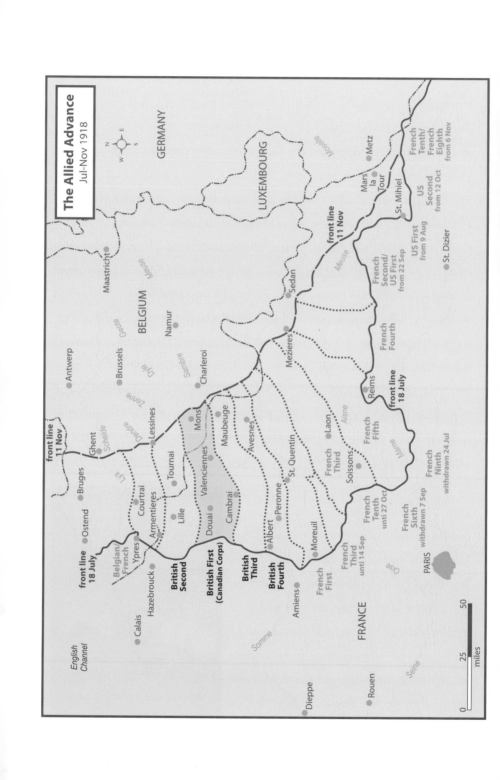

The Allied Advance
Jul-Nov 1918

GERMANY

N
W E
S

LUXEMBOURG

Moselle

Metz

Mars la Tour

St. Mihiel

US Second from 12 Oct

French Tenth/ French Eighth from 6 Nov

front line 11 Nov

Meuse

US First from 9 Aug

French Second/ US First from 22 Sep

St. Dizier

Maastricht

BELGIUM

Geer

Meuse

Sedan

Namur

Mezieres

French Fourth

Antwerp

Brussels

Dyle

Zenne

Sambre

Charleroi

Reims

front line 18 July

Aisne

Laon

French Fifth

front line 11 Nov

Ghent

Scheldt

Dender

Lys

Lessines

Mons

Maubeuge

Avesnes

St. Quentin

French Third

Soissons

Marne

French Ninth withdrawn 24 Jul

Bruges

Courtrai

Armentieres

Tournai

Lille

Valenciennes

Douai

Cambrai

Albert

Peronne

Moreuil

French Tenth until 27 Oct

French Sixth withdrawn 7 Sep

Oise

PARIS

front line 18 July

Ostend

Ypres

Belgian/ French

Hazebrouck

British Second

British First (Canadian Corps)

British Third

British Fourth

Amiens

French Third until 14 Sep

French First

Calais

Somme

FRANCE

Dieppe

Rouen

Seine

English Channel

miles
0   25   50

The Hundred Days: Arras to Mons 1918

After Currie and Rawlinson persuaded Haig to close down the Amiens offensive, Sir Julian Byng's Third Army began an advance north of the Somme towards Bapaume. Byng was hesitant, convinced that German reinforcements would block an Amiens-like breakthrough, so he adopted a bite and hold approach which proved highly effective. Pausing to consolidate after securing minor gains his British forces, plus the New Zealand Division, inflicted heavy casualties when the Germans counterattacked. The next day Third Army renewed the attack, overwhelming the defenders and taking 10,000 prisoners. Known as the "Battle of Albert" its success, coming on the heels of Amiens and Tenth French Army's five mile advance on the British flank, led Haig to send an extraordinary message to his army commanders. The enemy, he insisted, "has not the means to deliver counterattacks on an extended scale nor has he the numbers to hold a position against the very extended advance which is now be directed upon him" by all the Allied armies. "Risks which a month ago would have been criminal ought now to be incurred as duty." It was, Haig believed, the return of open warfare

Alfred Theodore Joseph Bastien, *Cavalry and Tanks at Arras, 1918*. [CWM 19710261-0090]

Arras and breaking the DQ line - 26 August - 2 September 1918

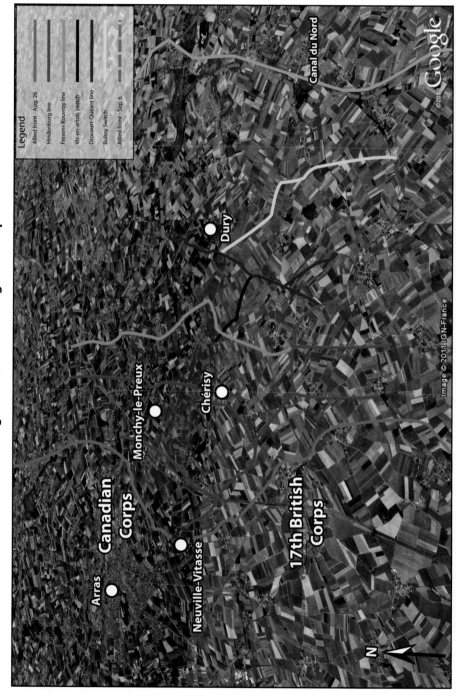

Legend

Allied front - Aug. 26

Hindenburg line

Fresnes Rouvroy line

Vis-en-artois switch

Drocourt-Quéant line

Bullsy Switch

Allied front - Sep. 6

Canal du Nord

Dury

Chérisy

Monchy-le-Preux

Neuville-Vitasse

Arras

Canadian Corps

17th British Corps

N

Image © 2011 IGN-France

©2010 Google

where divisions would act "independently of its neighbour advancing to distant objectives."

Fortunately, British Army commanders were used to Haig's bursts of optimism and ignored his instructions. If the battlefield became more open, different tactics could be employed but no experienced Corps commander would cease to use his artillery as the principal weapon and none would order divisions to act independently. Haig's dream of using the Cavalry Corps to gain "strategic objectives" remained just a fantasy.

Haig's orders now called for "an advance by all troops on all fronts" drawing Fourth Army back into combat. The Canadians were returning to Horne's First Army in the Arras sector so Rawlinson was left with Third British Corps and the Australians. Between 24 August and 1 September the Australians led an advance that took them across the Somme and onto Mont St. Quentin hill north of Péronne that dominated the area. Péronne itself fell the next day.

The initial task assigned to the Canadian Corps was to overcome the German defences based on a series of hills. Historian Colonel Nicholson described the scene, which included the previously bloodied heights of Monchy-le-Preux:

> The enemy's main defence positions, supplemented by various subsidiary switches and strong points, were among the strongest on the Western Front. The ground was pocked with the scars of 1917 and early 1918, and in the litter of old trenches and fortifications German engineers had found ready-made positions which they had considerably strengthened. Furthermore, topography was on the side of the Germans. The battle area spread over the north-eastern slopes of the Artois Hills, whose summits about Monchy were over three hundred feet above the valley-bottoms of the Scarpe and the Sensée. The latter river, flowing generally eastward, together with its tributaries had dissected the hills into numerous deep valleys. The intervening ridges and high points, often mutually supporting, the enemy had fortified with a skill that demonstrated his mastery in military engineering. (Great War Historian Colonel Nicholson)

Known as the Battle of the Scarpe, the operation began at 0300 hours 26 August 1918 with fourteen brigades of field artillery, and nine heavy brigades. There were few tanks available after the losses east of Amiens and just nine were allotted to each of the two divisions leading the attack.

Advancing during the attack on the Hindenburg Line. [NAS (18) L.1204]

North of the Arras-Cambrai road, the centre-line of the Corps advance, Third Canadian Division seized the hills including Monchy in less than five hours, an extraordinary feat testifying to the weakness of the enemy and the skill of the Canadians in a night attack.

The Second Division also made good initial progress but orders to shift the weight to the southeast, capturing the Wancourt Ridge, to assist Third Army slowed the advance to the division's objectives. After a night of heavy rain both Canadian divisions made some progress against determined opposition, advancing five miles while overcoming the remaining defences of the Fresnes-Rouvroy system. The actions cost the Canadians close to 6,000 men, a taste of what was to come at the Drocourt-Quéant or D-Q Line.

Casualties to British and Dominion formations were now causing grave concern. The British War Cabinet sent a telegram to Haig (29 August) warning against incurring heavy casualties in the next weeks as infantry reinforcements for the British Expeditionary Force were simply not available. Due to conscription and the cancellation of exemptions, the Canadians were the only one of Haig's Corps able to restore formations to full strength. This inevitably meant that Currie would be asked to take the lead in a series of costly assaults. The situation was dramatised when 4th British Division, which had fought under Currie in the second phase of the late August advance, reported that only one brigade was fit for action against the D-Q Line, forcing the Canadians to take an even larger share of the assault.

Breaking through the D-Q Line required detailed planning and lots of artillery. There was little opportunity for any kind of "open warfare." Five brigades followed a rolling barrage would have to overcome three defensive lines before reaching the ground overlooking the Canal du Nord. Currie decided to attack at dawn hoping that the Mark V tanks could move forward with the infantry at zero hour. By the end of the day, seven Canadians had won the Victoria Cross and the D-Q had been breached on a 7,000 yard front. The next morning the enemy was gone, retreating behind the Canal du Nord. Over 6,000 German soldiers were in Corps prisoner of war cages and many more were killed or wounded, at a cost of some 5,600 Canadian casualties.

The successful assault on the D-Q Line, the most complete defensive system on the Western Front, was supported by a parallel British-Australian advance to Bapaume, forcing a German retreat all along the front. The German withdrawal and the exhaustion of the Allied armies slowed the operational tempo but Third British Army resumed the advance on 12 September and Fourth Army joined in six days later. On 25 September a large-scale Franco-American offensive on a 44-

Original caption reads: 'The famous Canal du Nord which the Canadians stormed. Canadian transport passing through it up to the fighting at BOURLON WOOD.' [NAS (182) X.25013]

Crossing the Canal du Nord & Bourlon Wood - 27 September 1918

Legend

Allied front

German front

Canal du Nord

Haynecourt

22nd British Corps

Marquion Line

Bourlon

Bourlon Wood

Canadian Corps

Inchy-en-Artois

7th British Corps

N

Image © 2011 IGN-France

©2010 Google

mile front began. The next day First Army joined in crossing the Canal du Nord and seizing Bourlon Wood. General Henry Horne, who commanded First Army, has been described as "a rather shadowy figure for historians … eclipsed by the prominence given to Sir Arthur Currie, his Canadian subordinate." Horne seemed content to leave the planning and conduct of operations to Currie which meant the Canadians did most of the heavy lifting in First Army.

Currie decided to advance on a narrow front, less than 2,500 yards, where the Canal du Nord was under construction and still dry. The enemy had strengthened defences in the area with dense belts of barbed wire but there was little protection from the kind of bombardment Corps and Army artillery could apply. Beyond the canal a second defensive position, the Marquion Line, crossed the front. The main objective, the high ground at Bourlon Wood, was to be attacked after 4th Canadian Division had crossed the canal to add weight to the advance.

A massive creeping barrage mixing smoke, shrapnel and high explosive led the way. Once again the Canadians overwhelmed the defenders and in less than five hours Bourlon Wood was under attack. Air support and superb work by the

Original caption reads: 'A Dug-out fire in Bourlon Wood. An 8.3 German Howitzer blown over by the explosion of a dump near it. Good Canadian artillery fire is sure proof here.' [NAS (194) X.25030]

Battle of Cambrai - 28 September - 11 October 1918

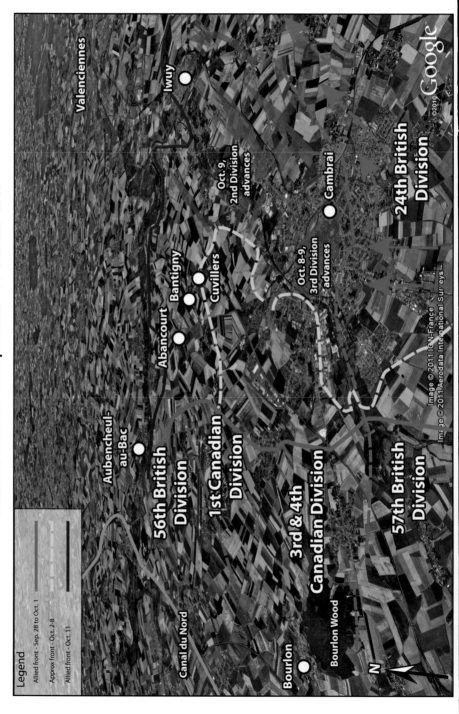

engineers who bridged the canal helped to maintain momentum and by nightfall leading elements were probing the last fortified positions in front of Cambrai. Unfortunately the Germans were determined to hold the city and the Escaut canal line as long as possible, and the battle for Cambrai turned into a bitter, attritional struggle.

After a failed attack by the 4th Division, Currie ordered the Corps to stage a new set-piece attack on 1 October. After initial progress enemy resistance stiffened and then a series of German counterattacks forced withdrawals. For the moment, the enemy had stabilized the front. Cambrai, badly damaged by shelling and arson, was finally cleared on 9 October after Third Army succeeded in crossing the canal south of the city, threatening a double envelopment. The Canadians fought their way into Cambrai, overcoming rearguards and dealing with mines and booby-traps. On 11 October the Corps was sent into reserve. The summary offered by the official historian states:

> Its casualties were many but by First World War standards not excessive in light of their task. The total officially reported killed, wounded, and missing between 22 August and 11 October numbered

Original caption reads: 'A Canadian leaving a hole in CAMBRAI with some rare souvenirs. They were new and no doubt were to be used during the victorious march into PARIS which so far has not taken place.' [NAS (190) X.25023]

Cyril Henry Barraud, *The Stretcher-bearer.* [CWM 19710261-0019]

1,544 officers and 29,262 other ranks. In achieving its victory the Corps had captured 18,585 prisoners, together with 371 guns and nearly 2,000 machine guns. Besides depriving the enemy of the great distributing centre of Cambrai, the Canadians had liberated 54 towns and villages standing on more than 116 square miles of French soil.

Cambrai was a complex battle fought on the outskirts and eventually the streets of an industrial city. No historian has examined this operation in any detail – an important task for the future. From Cambrai the Corps advanced to Valenciennes and Mons in the last month of the war. The story of the final advance needs to be understood in the context of the German effort to achieve an Armistice which would preserve the Kaiser's regime, the prestige of the German Army, and as many territorial conquests as possible.

On 10 September, the German High Command agreed to permit an approach to the Allies through the Queen of the Netherlands. This gambit was abandoned when on 14 September the Austrian Emperor, fearing the complete disintegration of his armies, issued a public appeal for a peace conference in a neutral state. This transparent attempt to preserve a collapsing empire followed by a public declaration of German war aims that called for preserving the Treaty of Brest-Litovsk, the return of all German colonies, and effective control of Belgium.

President Wilson's reply to the Austrian peace note included his enunciation of five essential conditions for peace, an elaboration of the famous "Fourteen Points." He added words that forced Germany's leaders to rethink their claims. Wilson declared "there can be no peace obtained by any bargain or compromise with the Governments of the Central Empires." The next day Bulgaria, one of the four Central Powers, surrendered. Ludendorff subsequently wrote that 28 September was the day he knew "the war was now lost…If we had the strength to reverse the situation in the West, then of course nothing would yet have been lost. But we had not the means…We had to count on being beaten back again and again."

Insisting that "every hour of delay is dangerous," Ludendorff led an effort to reconstitute the German government and issue an immediate call for an end to the fighting. A new Chancellor, Prince Max of Baden, was appointed on 4 October and "with a view to avoiding further bloodshed" he signed a letter to President Wilson requesting an immediate Armistice.

Wilson's reply, 8 October, demanded immediate "withdrawal of their forces everywhere from invaded territory" – not the response the German government was hoping for. On 12 October the Germans agreed to evacuate occupied territory but with an international commission supervising the process.

Any chance of a conciliatory response from Wilson or other Allied leaders was diminished by the sinking of the Irish Mail Boat *RMS Leinster* on 10 October. Over 500 men, women, and children including soldiers returning from leave were drowned in this pointless U-boat attack. Wilson echoed the public outcry, insisting on 14 October that "there can be no peace as long as Germany attacks passenger ships."

The small coterie of decision-makers in Germany were divided and uncertain. Ludendorff wanted to avoid any responsibility for a military surrender while Crown Prince Rupprecht warned that "we must obtain peace before the enemy breaks through into Germany…"

Prince Max crafted a new note on 20 October accepting the need to have military advisors determine the details of the Armistice as long as no demands were made "that would be irreconcilable with the honour of the German people and with paving the way to a peace of justice." He did promise to end the sinking of passenger ships.

Wilson now proposed what amounted to unconditional surrender which provoked another crisis in Germany. This led to both the dismissal of Ludendorff

Battle of Valenciennes - 1-11 October 1918

Legend

- Canadian lines - Nov. 1
- Front line night - Nov. 2
- Army boundries

12th Canadian Infantry Battalion

Valenciennes

Night assault 1-2 October

4th Canadian Division

Mont Houy

49th British Division

Famars

N

Image © 2010 IGN-France
Image © 2011 Aerodata International Surveys

©2010 Google

Murder on the High Seas by the Kaiser's Minions

and a statement on from the German government on 26 October that it awaited "proposals for an Armistice." Despite this public admission of defeat, orders for a last sortie to save the honour of the navy were issued. The sailors mutinied and as Germany slipped into chaos the Kaiser fled to Holland.

Neither the British nor the French governments had finalized a decision on the exact terms of an Armistice and soon events made such discussion irrelevant. The Turkish Government sent envoys to sign a separate peace on 26 October and Austria soon followed. On 5 November Marshal Ferdinand Foch was authorized to "receive representatives of the German Government and communicate to them the terms of the Armistice." The terms, amounting to unconditional surrender were presented on 8 November in a railway carriage in the Forêt de Compiègne. The German delegates were given 22 hours until 1100 hours on 11 November to sign the Armistice. No representative of the German Army was present in a deliberate attempt to place blame for the debacle on civilians.

The prolonged Armistice negotiations had little impact on Allied military operations raising the age-old question of the legitimacy or wisdom of continuing combat when the war is all but won. This issue became particularly important to Canadians after Sir Arthur Currie was criticized for the unnecessary deaths of Canadian soldiers. Rumours, innuendo and specific attacks on his reputation by

Mons - 11 November 1918

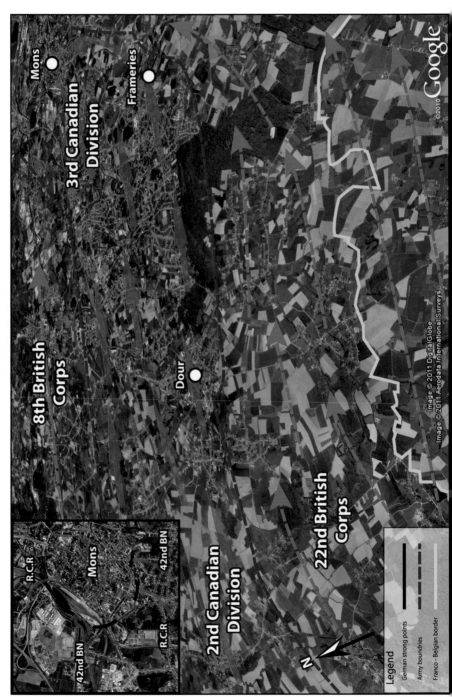

Sam Hughes, during and after the war, culminated in the famous trial in Port Hope where Currie defended his reputation and won a form of vindication in 1928.

Currie consistently argued that the Canadian Corps had been following explicit orders as it advanced towards Mons. Certainly the last large set-piece attack of the war for Canadians, the Battle of Valenciennes, was the result of a directive from Haig to General Horne to capture the city. This attack was to be carried out simultaneously with attacks by Third and Fourth Armies. The 51st Highland Division, part of 17th British Corps, began the attack with an assault on 28 October, but were unable to hold the ground gained.

Canadian troops storming fortifications at Valenciennes. [NAS (189) X.25021]

The Canadian Corps took over employing the heaviest artillery bombardment in support of single brigade ever tried during the war. The 10th Brigade swept over Mont Houy, capturing stunned prisoners and reaching the edge of the city. Brigadier Andrew McNaughton, then serving as the senior Corps artillery officer, described the artillery program: "The barrage and bombardment had left scarcely a yard of ground untouched...the Canadian Corps had paid the price of victory ... in shells and not in life." Casualties were less than 400 with 80 killed in action. The next day the enemy abandoned Valenciennes.

The Second Canadian Division led the advance to Mons with orders to capture it if it could be done "without many casualties." Was the decision to maintain pressure based on the symbolism of Mons where the war, for the British Expeditionary Force, had begun?

Currie was to say that "it would be befitting that the capture of Mons should close the fighting records of the Canadian Troops" but the reality was that all the leading divisions continued operations through to 11 November. No Allied commander was willing to allow the enemy time to regroup and delay an Armistice.

Frederick Varley, *For What?* [CWM 19710261-0770]

Notes on Battlefield Touring

Your trip will usually begin at Charles de Gaulle airport. We have found that arriving a day ahead and staying in an airport hotel with a sidetrip into Paris and an early night allows us to overcome jetlag and start on the battlefield tour in good shape. The airport hotels located at Terminal 2, Ibis, Novotel and Sheraton are the easiest to use but complementary transport to the less expensive and more varied hotels on the edge of the airport in Roissy-en-France is available from all terminals. If you do decide to travel into Paris, you can take the RER train from Terminal 2. Outside of rush hour a taxi may be a better option, especially if you are staying at a hotel in Roissy.

We suggest you invest in a good GPS. Many car rental agencies will have them for rent but the price works out to be virtually the same as it is to buy. Many of the newer models are fully functional in Europe and North America. For your convenience we have placed in brackets beside each tour stop the exact address of each location (or its immediate vicinity). A number of GPS units have loaded attractions including a historical section that will sometimes have the exact area as well as a few sites you may want to visit. In Europe, where gas stations are not as plentiful as in North America, the GPS will also let you know where you can find fuel. Lodging and dining options are also available. Be sure to note the location and availability of all washrooms.

Although most of the historical monuments and cemeteries are well marked, the signs can also be easy to miss. They are usually slightly lower than signs in North America. Once you become familiar with their placement and appearance, however, you will notice them quite easily. Finally, the tours make for rather full days and have been designed in such a way as to include a number of sites.

Feel free to use this guidebook as a set of suggestions and depart from its recommendations as you see fit. Absolute must-see areas of the tour have been highlighted. In the end, the only way to cater to both the passing tourist and the military enthusiast was to make it as wide-ranging as possible.

TOUR

Touring the Ieper salient

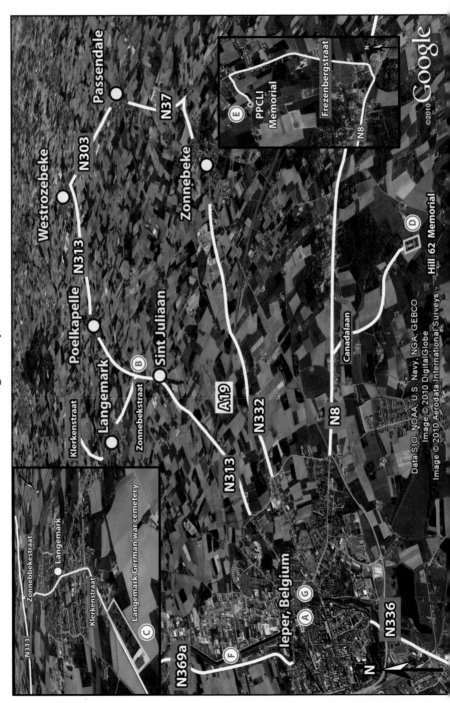

Passendale
N37
N303
Westrozebeke
N313
Poelkapelle
N313
Klerkenstraat
Langemark
Zonnebekstraat
B
Sint Juliaan
A19
N313
N332
Zonnebeke

PPCLI
Memorial
E
Frezenbergstraat
N
N8

D
Hill 62 Memorial

Canadalaan

N8

Langemark
Zonnebekestraat
Klerkenstraat
Langemark German war cemetery
C
N313
N369a

Ieper, Belgium
A
G
F
N336
N

Data SIO, NOAA, U.S. Navy, NGA, GEBCO
Image © 2010 DigitalGlobe
Image © 2010 Aerodata International Surveys
©2010 Google

After picking up the rental vehicle, follow the signs for "Autres Directions" then take the A1 autoroute north, "Direction Lille." This offers a trouble free drive away from the morning traffic in the Paris area. Your first stop should be *L'Historial de la Première Guerre Mondiale*. It is an outstanding museum and exhibition centre in Péronne, (A1 exit 13) follow the signs to L'Historial. There is free parking and local cafés for coffee or lunch. The museum provides an introduction to the military and cultural history of the Great War and features among other powerful exhibits the entire *Der Krieg* collection of drawings by Otto Dix, a German Expressionist painter who portrayed the agony of trench warfare in graphic images. There is also an excellent video on the Battle of the Somme that is well worth watching (www.historial.org).

From Péronne, Ieper (spelled Ypres during the war) is a two-hour drive. We prefer to stay in the Novotel (GPS – Sint Jacobsstraat 15, 8900 Ieper, Belgium) which is a short walk from the Menin Gate and the Cloth Hall but there are a number of other hotels in the centre of town including the Albion and Ambrosia.

Inside L'Historial, Peronne, France. [Nick Lachance]

The Ariane is a more expensive choice with its own excellent restaurant. For Canadians there are some must-see sites in the Ypres area.

A Begin your tour in the Main Square and visit the "In Flanders Fields" Museum in the famous Cloth Hall. The museum offers a multi-media introduction to a late 20th century interpretation of the Great War as a plague-like tragedy. The exhibits speak to the way in which soldiers and civilians experienced a war which apparently just happened to take place in this part of Belgium. As you enter you can obtain a card to insert at various computer terminals. The card identifies a soldier or civilian and you then follow their individual experience during the war.

B Next head northeast on the N313 to the "Brooding Soldier" Memorial at Vancouver Corner in Sint Julian (GPS – Brugseweg 123, 8920 Langemark, Belgium). The French names in this part of Belgium have been changed to reflect the language of the Flemish majority so on most signs and maps St. Julien is Saint Juliaan. Here the Canadian Corps faced the first use of poisonous gas by the German Army at the Battle of Second Ypres in 1915. The sculpture, designed by Canadian Frederick Clemsha, is surrounded by cedar trees that are trimmed in the shape of shells.

C Take time to visit the famous German military cemetery at nearby Langemarck. Head northwest on the Zonnebekestraat directly adjacent

Langemarck German War Cemetery. [Matt Symes]

to the Brooding Soldier Monument. Follow the road through Langemarck-Poelkapelle where it changes to the Klerkenstraat. The cemetery is on the left (GPS – 8920 Langemarck-Poelkapelle, Belgium). Of note, the student battalion that was decimated by British rifle fire during the German attack on Ypres in October 1914 are buried here (One of the large blocks to the far right when you enter). It is an event remembered in Germany as the *Kindermord*, or "Massacre of the Innocents." There is some debate but the bunkers in the cemetery are

"The Grieving Elders". [Matt Symes]

thought to have been constructed between Second Ypres (April 1915) and Third Ypres (June 1917) and were once part of the Hindenburg-Line that ran between Langemarck and Geluveld. They were restored for the official opening in 1932. There is a famous video clip of Adolf Hitler visiting this cemetery in 1940 on his tour through occupied Belgium and France. For those interested in war and memory, a trip north to the Vladslo German War Cemetery is strongly recommended (GPS - Houtlandstraat 3, 8600 Diksmuide, Belgium). Here the famed "The Grieving Elders" sculptures by Käthe Kollwitz watches over her youngest son Peter and over 25,643 German war dead.

D The next key location is the Canadian Memorial on Hill 62 at the end of a purpose-built road called the Canadalaan. (GPS – Canadalaan 26, 8902 Ypres, Belgium). From the Langemark Cemetery retrace your steps southeast to the N313. Continue south until you reach the N345 and turn left. Follow the N345 until you reach the N8 exit direction Meenseweg. Canadalaan, which is lined with maple trees, is less than a kilometre on your right. The Memorial is at the end of the road. On a clear day the strategic importance of Hill 62 is evident. The Canadian action to recapture the high ground denied the German Army a clear

Battlefield remnants on display at the Sanctuary Wood Museum. [Nick Lachance]

view into Ypres. To the northwest the Cloth Hall stands out on the horizon. It is highly recommended that you visit the privately owned Sanctuary Wood Museum with its assorted collection of First World War ordnance, a network of trenches and shell craters to walk around, and a chance for coffee and a washroom break.

E About 10 minutes from Hill 62, in Frezenberg, lies the more obscure and less visited memorial to the Princess Patricia's Canadian Light Infantry

The Memorial to the Princess Patricias Canadian Light Infantry. [Matt Symes]

(GPS – 38 Frezenberstraat, Zonnebeke, Vlaams Gewest, Belgium will take you to where you turn left at the Princess Patriciastraat). At the end of Canadalaan take a right on the N8. You will see signs for the monument that lead you onto Oude Kortrijkstraat on the left. Take your first left onto Frezenberstraat. Princess Patriciastraat will be on your left. The monument, on your right, is low to the ground and not well marked. The plaque reads "Here 8 May 1915 the "Originals" of Princess Patricia's Canadian Light Infantry commanded by their Founder Major A. Hamilton Gault, DSO, held firm and counted not the loss." As part of the BEF's 80th Brigade (nicknamed the "Stonewall Brigade" after its defence of Ypres), the Patricias suffered almost 400 casualties and were reduced to just four officers and 154 men at the end of the battle. Frezenberg is the graveyard of the original regiment and the Patricias first battle honour.

(F) Many Canadians make a point of visiting the Essex Farm Dressing Station and the British War Cemetery because of the association with Major John McCrae (GPS – John Mccraepad, 8900 Ieper, Belgium). Travel north along Frezenbergstraat to the A19 heading toward Veurne/Diksmuide/Poperinge. When the A19 ends, turn left at the N38 and follow the road across the Ieperlee Kanaal (formerly the Yser Canal) and take your first exit toward Diksmuiden. The Essex Farm Dressing Station and Cemetery are on your immediate left. Here

Essex Farm Cemetery. [Matt Symes]

overlooking the poppy-covered fields, McCrae composed *In Flanders Fields*. The Dressing Stations are preserved directly adjacent to the graveyard. Be sure to visit the grave of Rifleman Valentine Joe Strudwick, one of the youngest Commonwealth soldier killed in the Great War at the age of 15. His grave is always adorned with a number of little wooden Remembrance Crosses and is easy to spot.

(**G**) Finally, return to Ieper's main square. The ceremony at the Menin Gate with the playing of the Last Post at 8:00pm is not to be missed. The Menin Gate was designed by Sir Reginald Blomfield and unveiled July 1927 by Field Marshal Lord Plumer. To the thousands of bereaved parents who had come for the inauguration or who were listening by radio back in Great Britain, Plumer offered the consolation the memorial was meant to convey: "He is not missing; he is here." Later generations would reject such phrases and their implication of willing sacrifice, but despite Wilfrid Owen and other war poets, official commemoration in 1927 evoked the idea of "Death So Noble." The Menin Gate bears the names of 54,896 soldiers, including 6,940 Canadians who died in the Ypres Salient before 16 August 1917. With the exception of the German occupation during the Second World War, the ceremony has carried on every night uninterrupted, by the fire brigade of Ypres, since 2 July 1928. If you would like to take part in the ceremony you can purchase a wreath from the tourist information

The Menin Gate evening ceremony. [Matt Symes]

centre in the Cloth Hall (You will exit into this area after you have finished visiting the In Flander's Field Museum) and speak to those in charge who can be seen organizing the ceremony around 7:30pm.

While based in Ieper you will no doubt wish to explore the battlefields of the Passchendaele offensive, described later in the tour section. Ieper is a fascinating place to visit. While you are there be sure to dine in the main square and visit the British Grenadier bookshop near the Menin Gate. Steve Douglas, who owns the store, is the man behind the Maple Leaf Legacy project, providing online photographs of every Canadian war grave (www.mapleleaflegacy.ca). For more information on other areas to tour in the Ypres Salient visit http://www.greatwar. co.uk and for tourist information, the Battlefields 1918 website. Click on "Ypres Salient" then "Ypres Tourism."

A few of the 54, 896 names on Menin Gate. [Matt Symes]

Touring the Somme Valley

Touring the Somme

We have enjoyed staying in Amiens on several battlefield tours but we prefer to select a hotel in Arras for the two to four days devoted to the Somme, Vimy and the 1918 battles from Arras to Mons. We recommend the Ibis Centre in the heart of the city if you are on a tight budget. The Mercure Atria and Holiday Inn Express at the railway station plaza offer better, larger rooms. The Mercure has a pleasant restaurant with good food. *Les Trois Luppars* in the Grand Place offers a more traditional location and we have enjoyed staying here. The liveliest restaurant-café scene is in the *Place des Héros*, but if you are after better cuisine consider the *Faisanderie* or *Rapière* in the Grand Place. One disadvantage to staying in Arras is missing the cathedral in Amiens which is one of the glories of the Western world. Listed as a UNESCO World Heritage Site, this 13th century marvel is the largest cathedral in France. There are a number of plaques commemorating Canadian regiments and battles but the building speaks for itself. Amiens is a short drive west of Pozières. The cathedral is visible from the edge of the town and is well marked.

 For Canadians a visit to the Somme must begin at the Newfoundland Memorial Park at Beaumont-Hamel (GPS – 80300 D73, Auchonvillers,

Students on the Cleghorn Battlefield tour visit Beaumont-Hamel. [Nick Lachance]

France). From Arras, take the D917 south to the D929 which bypasses Baupaume, continue west on the D929 to Pozières then right at the Canadian sign to Beaumont-Hamel. You will pass by Thiepval and the Ulster Tower before reaching the well-marked park where Canadian university students will greet you and offer a guided tour or a detailed map for a self-guided walk. Be sure to walk up to the top of the monument for a good view over the battlefield. As you walk through no-man's-land to the cemetery, you will come across the Danger Tree encased in cement. It is the only known original tree in No-Man's Land to survive the fighting north of the Albert-Bapaume road during the war. Soldiers used this tree to guide themselves back to their own positions after night raids. The Germans, who knew this, used this lone mark to range their guns, hence the nickname "Danger Tree." In Y Ravine Cemetery look for the Caribou Regimental Insignia of the Newfoundland Regiment. As the path turns slightly left you will see Y Ravine –

The German front line. There is also a large monument to the 51st Scottish Highlanders on the grounds overlooking Y Ravine and the scene of their successful assault on the German defences 13 November 1916. Look across the farmer's field and you will see a clump of trees in the distance. Note how their tops are level with the farming ground. These are the trees that have grown in Hawthorn Crater (if you continue northwest along the D73 and take the first right down a farmer's road to get to the site as well as Hawthorn Ridge Cemetery No. 1).

The Danger Tree. [Nick Lachance]

TOUR

Thurston Topham, *Night Scene On The Somme.* [CWM 19710261-0735]

B The next major action of the Canadian Corps on the Somme is Courcelette but there are some worthwhile stops along the way. The Ulster Tower Memorial commemorates the 36th Ulster Division (GPS – 80300 D73, Thiepval, France). Continue back along the D73 toward Pozières and you cannot miss the tower on your left. The monument is nearly an identical replica of Helen's Tower in Bangor, County Down, Northern Ireland which stood on the estate where many of the men of the Ulster Division trained before heading to France. An audio/visual presentation explains the initial success of the Ulster Division on 1 July 1916 and illustrates their isolation before a forced withdrawal. There is a small café, bookstore, and washrooms. Please note, it is closed on Sundays and Mondays.

Ulster Tower. [Matt Symes]

TOUR

C Continuing toward Pozières on the D73, the Thiepval Memorial is the British "Vimy" (GPS – Rue de L'Ancre, 80300 Thiepval, France). Standing 45 metres high with the names of 73,367 British soldiers who have no known grave listed on the pillars, Thiepval is the largest British War Memorial in the world. More than 90 percent of the names listed died between July and November 1916. At the foot of the memorial 300 British and 300 French soldiers, are buried together to commemorate the joint nature of the 1916 offensive. In 2004 an impressive interpretation centre run by the British Legion opened.

Thiepval Memorial at the Unveiling in 1932.

D As you make your way to the Courcelette battlefields along the D73 it is worth a brief stop at Mouquet Farm (GPS – la Ferme du Mouquet, 8300, Ovilliers-la-Boisselle, France). Over the course of August and early September the Australians managed to reach the farm three times but were forced back each time as German artillery rained down on them from the three sides of the salient. The Canadian Corps were sent in relief on 5 September 1916 and the farm was not captured until 27 September. There is a detailed plaque with a battle map at the beginning of the outstretched farm road.

The monument at Mouquet Farm. The line of trees are located in the distance is the approximate location where the Canadians took over for the Australians. [Eric McGeer]

E For those interested in the First Australian Division Monument in Pozières and the viewing platform looking over the battlefield take a right on Rue de L'Église just before the D929 (GPS – 333 Rue de L'Église, 8300 Pozières, France). As the road veers toward the D929 the monument will be on your right. The viewing platform that clearly illustrates the sweeping views the Germans held over the advancing Allied troops is across the road.

F To visit the Courcelette battlefields, head east on the D929. On the edge of Pozières you will find a memorial to the men of the tank Corps (GPS – 977 Route de Baupaume, 8300 Contalmaison, France). The monument commemorates the first use of the 'landships' in battle with scale models of the tanks used here in 1916. Across the road, the Windmill Memorial to the First Australian Division provides a good vantage point to survey the ground over which the Canadians fought in the fall of 1916. Directly ahead on the left side of the highway is the "Sugar Factory," rebuilt after the war on the original site. The steeple of the church in Courcelette is visible as is the rising ground beyond that gave the Germans an overview of the preparations for the advance to Courcelette.

TOUR

The Courcelette Tank Monument. [Nick Lachance]

G The Canadian block Memorial for the 1916 Somme battles is about 800 metres further northeast on the D929 before the village of Courcelette (GPS – N Route Nationale, 8300 Martinpuich, France will take you to the Sugar Factory from which you cannot miss the Canadian Memorial). Parking is available across the highway.

H The village of Courcelette was completely destroyed in 1916 but has been largely rebuilt on the original footprint. Continue beyond the village to the Courcelette British cemetery (GPS – 42 Rue du Grand Chemin, 8300 Courcelette France). From the monument take a left onto the D107. Take your second left onto Rue du Chapitre which will turn into Gr. Grand Rue and guide directly to the cemetery. There are 1,970 Commonwealth soldiers buried here including 16-year-old Private George Ritchie from the Royal Canadian Dragoons and 17-year-old John Robertson from the 43rd Battalion Canadian Infantry, Manitoba Regiment. If you walk along the edges of the farm track continuing beyond the cemetery with a keen eye you will still find shell casings, shrapnel, and other bits of ordnance from the war. The German trench line the Canadians called "Regina" crossed the road just beyond the cemetery.

Regina Trench Cemetery, located on the site of the actual German earthworks, is north of the village in the middle of farmland and is well marked. Retrace your steps back to Courcelette about 700 metres and take a left and continue northwest for about 1.5 kilometres. The original cemetery, where the graves are closer, was put together in the winter of 1916-1917. There are now more than 2,000 Commonwealth soldiers buried here including American pilot Lieutenant Ervin Shaw. Shaw's gravestone is directly beside his observer, Sergeant Thomas Smith, in what is a common practice to bury aircrew in graves that virtually touch each other.

You will want to visit Adanac Cemetery (Canada spelled backwards) on the D107 between Courcelette and Miraumont (GPS – D107, 8300 Courcelette, France. This point will take you to the edge of Courcelette on the D107 headed toward the cemetery 1.3 kilometres north). Adanac cemetery is the final resting place of 1,072 Canadians among the 3,186 men buried here. Among the Canadians, Private (Piper) James Richardson is buried here. The 20-year-old from Chilliwack B.C. was awarded the Victoria Cross for playing his company over the top. As the company approached Regina Trench they came under intense

A view of the Somme Battlefield north of the Hawthorn Crater. [Eric McGeer]

TOUR

Mary Riter Hamilton, *The Sadness of the Somme.* [LAC 1988-180-19]

fire and Piper Richardson "strode up and down outside the wire, playing his pipes with the greatest coolness…" His comrades "rushed the wire with such fury and determination that the obstacle was overcome and the position captured." Losses among the assault battalions were so heavy that the captured sections of Regina Trench could not be held. Richardson survived the battle but later died in an attempt to retrieve his pipes which he had laid down while helping a wounded soldier in no-man's-land. His pipes, which sat in a Scottish school unidentified for almost a century, were repatriated in 2006.

The 1916 battlefields of the Somme include some of the most visited sites in Northern France. Quite apart from regular tourists and tour busses, there will be numerous student tour groups shepherded by anxious teachers. Patience may be required. You may also want to visit The Somme Trench Museum (Musée des Abris - Somme 1916) in Albert, which focuses on the July 1916 offensive and the realities of trench warfare (http://www.somme-trench-museum.co.uk). A series of dioramas are presented in tunnels once used to shelter the inhabitants. The museum is located beside the Basilica in the centre of Albert (GPS - Rue Anicet Godin, 80300 Albert, France).

There are a few other locations not directly involving the Canadians that are worth seeing if you have the time. The South African Museum and National Memorial at Longueval was built in the Apartheid era as part of a public relations campaign. The features of the original are intact though the message has changed. The attached museum tells the story of the battle for Delville Wood (GPS – Route de Ginchy, 8360 Longueval, France). For those with a Welsh background the unique Red Dragon Memorial in commemoration of the 38th (Welsh) Division attacks on Mametz Wood is a must see. (GPS – Bois Santin, 8300 Bazentin, France. If you are coming from Pozières you will pass a Commonwealth cemetery on your right and if you are coming from Mametz the monument will be on your right). The Welsh Division suffered 4,000 casualties between 7 and 12 July 1916 but were ultimately successful in clearing the forested area. The famous poet Siegfried Sassoon fought in the engagement and modernist novelist David Jones wrote about the attack in his work "In Parenthesis." For information on other areas to see on the Somme battlefield visit: www.somme-battlefields.com.

The 38th (Welsh) Division Red Dragon Monument. The Dragon is facing Mametz Wood with its claws pointed fiercely toward the battleground. [Geordie Michael]

Touring Vimy

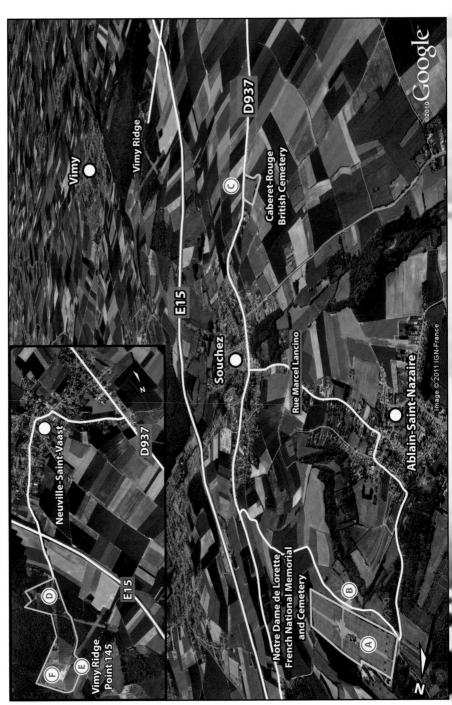

Vimy

Vimy Ridge

D937

E15

Souchez

Caberet-Rouge
British Cemetery

Rue Marcel Lancino

C

Ablain-Saint-Nazaire

Notre Dame de Lorette
French National Memorial
and Cemetery

B

A

N

Neuville-Saint-Vaast

D937

E15

Vimy Ridge
Point 145

D

E

F

N

Google ©2010

Image ©2011 IGN-France

Touring Vimy

(A) Begin your study of Vimy at Notre-Dame-de-Lorette (GPS – Colline de Notre-Dame-de-Lorette, 62153 Ablain-Saint-Nazaire, France). From Arras head north on the D937 to Souchez and turn left on the D57. Turn right at the Rue de la Blanc Voie and veer left at the fork continuing on the same road up the hill to the cemetery. It is well marked. This is the site of the French national cemetery and memorial for the battles of 1914-1915 and is well worth visiting in its own right. Over 45,000 French soldiers are buried in this cemetery. The crypt near the basilica contains the tombs of unknown soldiers from many French conflicts throughout history. At the far end of the cemetery (to your left from the main gates) you will find the Jewish and Muslim graves. The Muslim graves are tilted perfectly to Mecca and their uniqueness is worth the walk.

(B) To understand the battles for Vimy Ridge walk to the observation areas that overlook the battlefield. The gently sloping western side of the Vimy escarpment is laid out before you. The twin pylons of the memorial are visible on

The Muslim section of the cemetery at Notre-Dame-de-Lorette. [Matt Symes]

clear days 4 kilometres away and you can gain some idea of the scale of the Corps battle that was fought here.

The significance of the French Army's operations in the spring and fall of 1915 when the Tenth Army reached but could not hold Vimy Ridge will quickly be apparent. Without Allied control of the Lorette Spur and the withdrawal of the German defensive positions onto the ridge it is unlikely that any attack would have succeeded.

Orient yourself by identifying the Vimy Memorial at Point 145 and the jagged towers at Mont St. Eloi to the south. The map on p.54 highlights the sectors through which the four Canadian divisions attacked as well as the artillery positions on the Lorette Ridge and in the valley below. Each of these sectors can be explored if you have time but most visitors to Vimy need the better part of a day to visit the memorial, the tunnels and the interpretation centre.

(C) On your way to Vimy, Canadians may wish to take a slight detour to the impressive Cabaret Rouge War Cemetery (GPS – 1 Rue Carnot 62153 Souchez, France). Return to the D937 and retrace your steps through Souchez. The cemetery is on the edge of the town on your right. It is from this cemetery in 2000 that the remains of an unidentified Canadian soldier were exhumed and laid to rest within the Tomb of the Unknown Soldier in front of the War Memorial in Ottawa. Oliver and Wilfred Chenier, brothers from Buckingham, Quebec, who died on the first day of the Battle of Vimy Ridge are also buried here.

(D) You should start your tour of Vimy at the visitation centre taking time to explore the replica trenches and the underground tunnels (GPS – Route des Canadiens 62580 Thélus, France). From Cabaret Rouge Cemetery continue south on the D937 and turn left on Rue du 11 Novembers. Veer left on Rue du Carlin and another left on the D55. Cross the A26 and it turns into Route des Canadiens where the interpretation center is. If you are with a small group you can sign up on the day but if you are with a large group (more than 6) you will need a reservation to visit the tunnels. To book a tour go to the Veterans Affairs Canada website and click on the links or email vimy_memorial@vac-acc.gc.ca. The phone number in France is 33 321 58 5834. From Canada, dial 011 before the 33. It is not possible to purchase lunch in the park so remember to bring sandwiches which you will only be allowed to eat in the parking lot where there are a few picnic tables.

(E) Next drive to the parking lot by the memorial. Before you visit the monument take a moment to look across the road from the upper parking lot at the Moroccan Division Memorial. It commemorates the members of the French Moroccan Division who fought their way to this point in 1915.

(F) As you walk toward the Vimy Memorial, designed by Walter Allward, you cannot help but be impressed by its sheer size and beauty. Jonathan Vance, who wrote the award-winning study of the Canadian memory of the Great War *Death So Noble*, called Vimy "Canada's primary altar to the fallen of war." At the time Arthur Currie worried that the monument would overshadow other greater Canadian achievements even if he conceded that "there it was that the Canadian Corps first fought as a unit and, as its components were drawn from all parts of the country, Vimy may be considered as the first appearance of our young nation at war." That Point 145 is such a striking physical landscape played just as important a role in deciding the location for Allward's design.

The Twin columns of the Vimy Memorial represent France and Canada, partners in arms. As you approach the monument the male and female sculptures on the right and left represent *Mourning Parents*. The Statues at the top of the columns represent *Truth and Knowledge*. As you wrap about the monument you

The twin columns of the Vimy Memorial. [Nick Lachance]

see *Mother Canada* mourning her dead. In the middle of the two pillars sits the *Spirit of Sacrifice and the Passing of the Torch*. As you descend the stair case and look back at the monument from the grass you see what represents an impenetrable *Wall of Defence*. On the southern side you have the *Breaking of the Swords* and on the northern edge the *Sympathy of the Canadians for the Helpless*. In the middle sits the *Stone Sarcophagus* representing Canada's killed soldiers. Though there is a deeply religious feel to the Vimy Memorial, the direct references are subtle. The wall and pillars represented the top of a cross and the sunlight on the monument was meant to give the effect of a cathedral.

The 11,285 names of missing Canadians with no known grave around the base of the Vimy Memorial were not part of the original design. The addition of the names of the missing was one of several alterations to the original design of the monument. This change transformed Vimy into hallowed ground, an empty tomb and therefore a place of pilgrimage. Allward also agreed to modify his "Breaking the Sword" sculpture which originally included a German helmet crushed under the foot of one of the figures. This was done to avoid "militaristic imagery."

The names of the missing on the Vimy Memorial. [Nick Lachance]

The memorial was unveiled in 1936 with thousands of Canadian Veterans and their families present for the Vimy pilgrimage. The pilgrimage like the memorial

Mourning Parents: The Mother

Mourning Parents: The Father

Truth and Knowledge

Mother Canada

The Spirit of Sacrifice and Passing the Torch

The Wall of Defence

The Stone Sarcophagus

The Breaking of the Swords

Sympathy of the Canadians for the Helpless

A large crowd of French civilians and Canadian pilgrims gather for the dedication of the monument, 26 July 1936. [PA 148873]

was full of ambiguities. Was it a celebration of the achievement of the Canadian Corps or a ceremony mourning the missing? Did the presence of King Edward VIII suggest an imperial event solidifying Canada's relationship with Britain or a statement about an independent Canadian nation? Was the monument to be seen as a remonstrance against war or a warning to the enemies of democracy that Canada would again play its part in defending Britain and France against German aggression? It was all these things and more.

Of the more than 65,000 Canadians killed in the Great War, 7,000 are buried in 30 cemeteries within a 20 kilometre radius of the Vimy Memorial. It would be virtually impossible to visit every Canadian grave, but if you have time make your way to La Chaudière Military Cemetery (GPS - 3-5 Route Nationale, 62580 Vimy, France). The burial ground, which was originally called Vimy Canadian Cemetery No. 1, is shaped like an artillery shell. Among the 638 Canadian soldiers buried here is Victoria Cross recipient Private John George Pattison, 50th Canadian Infantry, (Alberta Regiment).

On your way back to Arras you might consider visiting one of the three divisional memorials, placed shortly after the battle to honour the part played by the Canadian Corps in taking and holding Vimy Ridge. The easiest to find is the monument to the Second Division on the western edge of Thélus at the junction of the D49 and the N17 (GPS – 32 Rue des Artilleurs Canadiens, Thélus, France).

Sir Arthur Currie, unveiling the Second Division Memorial erected by Canadian Artillery in memory of their fallen comrades during the Battle of Vimy Ridge, February 1918. [PA 2507]

Arras

A tour of the area immediately east and north of Arras is not really recommended as urbanization, traffic and the absence of memorials or viewing points make for a difficult day. If you are determined to see Hill 70 and Lens consult Norm Christie's guidebook *Other Canadian Battlefields of the Great War* in his "For King and Empire" series. For current information search for "Arras Tourism-Battlefields." The official site has hotel links and other tourist information.

You might wish to visit the Arras Memorial and Flying Services Memorial located two kilometres west of the railway station on Blvd. Charles de Gaulle. Follow signs for La Citadelle, in the Faubourg-d'Amiens Commonwealth Cemetery. The Arras Memorial commemorates the 34,718 British, New Zealand and South African troops who died in the Arras sector and who have no known graves. The Flying Services Memorial commemorates the airmen who died in Northern France including the 207 fatalities in April 1917. There are 153 Canadians buried in the cemetery. Make time for the underground museum Carrière Wellington which is open every day from 10:00am-12:30pm and 1:30-6:00pm. (http://www.carriere-wellington.com). It provides real insight into the lives of soldiers and civilians. The website offers links to hotels, restaurants, and other activities in the Arras region.

TOUR

Touring Passendale

Touring Passchendaele

It is quite impossible to obtain any sense of what the area looked like in 1917. The village (now spelled Passendale) has been completely rebuilt, not restored, and though the farm land still yields shells and other ordnance fragments from the war, the drainage has been restored and the landscape appears unscarred. When the Canadians entered the battle, the British-Australian frontline included the hamlet of Gravenstafel.

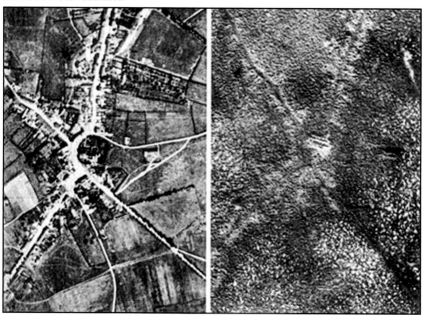

Passchendaele, before and after the battle.

(A) For those looking for a general overview of the battle begin your day at the "Passchendaele Memorial Museum" in Zonnebeke (GPS – Ieperstraat 5, B-8980 Zonnebeke). From Ieper take the N37 north to Zonnebeke and turn right on Berten Pilstraat where the museum is well marked. The Passchendaele Memorial Museum, located on the grounds of a rebuilt Chateau, has numerous artifacts and audio/visual presentations on the 1917 battle though the Canadian contribution is lumped in with the British forces. The trenches in the basement that greet visitors as they leave give an eerie claustrophobic feel that allows you to experience a bit of what it must have been like during the Great War. Consult the website for hours and events (http://www.passchendaele.be).

B The Canadian Memorial for the battle is located west of the village on the Canadalaan (GPS – Route 66 bvba Canadalaan 39, near 8980 Passendale, Belgium). Return to the N37/N332 heading north and turn left on the N303 north toward the centre of Passendale. Take a moment and stop at the Church in the centre of Passendale that has striking stained glass windows dedicated to the British 66th Division. Two impressive bronze plaques describing the various battles in the salient and providing information on the battle for Passchendaele are located in the square beside the church.

C Continue along Canadalaan which will take you directly to the Canadian bloc Memorial. The inscription reads "The Canadian Corps in Oct-Nov 1917 advanced across this valley, then a treacherous morass – captured and held Passchendaele Ridge." It is possible to look back to the spires of Ypres from the memorial, a sharp reminder of just how limited the advance was.

The Canadian Memorial at Passchendaele. [Matt Symes]

Among those who died in the battle to seize the ridge was Major Talbot Mercer Papineau who had publicly debated the meaning of the war and Canada's national identity with his cousin, the French Canadian nationalist Henri Bourassa. In an open letter to Bourassa, who was opposed to further Canadian participation in the war, Papineau declared that "French and English Canadians are fighting and dying side by side…Is their sacrifice to go for nothing or will it not cement a foundation for a true Canadian nation,…independent in thought, independent in action, independent even in its political organization – but in spirit united for high international and humane

Captain Talbot Papineau, 1916. [CWM EO-0476]

purposes to the two Motherlands of England and France?" Later in the letter he argued that "As a [French] minority in a great English-speaking continent,… we must rather seek to find points of contact and of common interest than points of friction and separation." Words that also needed to be addressed to English-speaking Canadians. Despite having secured a position behind the lines working for Canadian War Records Office, Major Papineau felt obligated to rejoin his battalion, the Princess Patricia's Canadian Light Infantry, in 1917. On October 30, moments before going over the top, Papineau's uttered his final recorded words to Major Hugh Wilderspin: "You know, Hughie, this is suicide." As you move to the 85th (Nova Scotia Highlanders) Battalion Memorial you will pass by Papineau's wartime makeshift grave that was lost to the carnage of Passchendaele.

(D) The 85th (Nova Scotia) Battalion Monument is located down a grass track on the south edge of the village off the N303/N37 toward Tyne-Cot (GPS – Passendalestraat 80, 8980 Passendale, Belgium). The location, on the left hand side, is not well marked and easily missed. The monument was originally raised in 1919 by the regiment before returning home. It was erected on the site of the battalion's headquarters during the battle. It commemorates the 85th Battalion's

Mary Riter Hamilton, *Canadian Monument Near Passchendaele.* [LAC 1988-180-114]. This painting features the Monument to the 85th (Nova Scotia) Battalion which stands atop the high ground south of the village and the final objective of the Passchendaele offensive.

costliest action of the war where the "Neverfails" as they became known, lost 148 men. A new monument, a replica of the original but made of Nova Scotia granite, was rededicated in 2001.

(E) End your visit at Tyne Cot Cemetery, the largest Commonwealth war cemetery in the world and the only one in which the Cross of Sacrifice is located on top of a German pill-box (GPS – Tynecotstraat 29, 8980 Zonnebeke, Belgium). Continue south on the N303/N37 and turn right on Tynecotstraat. The visitation center and the parking lot is well-marked on your right. Looking to the northeast, you can survey the approaches to the ridge. The Visitor Centre opened in 2007 serves to individualize the more than 200,000 Commonwealth casualties suffered at Passchendaele. The northeast boundary of the cemetery features the memorial to the missing with 34,887 names of British and New Zealand men who were killed after 16 August 1917 with no known grave. It was at Tyne Cot cemetery, near the end of his of his pilgrimage, that King George V said in a speech, "I have many times asked myself whether there can be more potent advocates of peace upon earth through the years to come, than this massed

An aerial view of Tyne Cot Cemetery. [Eric McGeer]

multitude of silent witnesses to the desolation of war." Of the 11,954 burials, 8,367 – 70 percent of the total – are unidentified and inscribed with the haunting epitaph "Known unto God." Of the remaining 30 percent, there are two that visitors will want to locate. The grave of Arthur Conway Young, Second Lieutenant with the Royal Irish Fusiliers, carries the simple but potent anti-war message "Sacrificed to the fallacy that war can end war." Canadians will want to find the grave of Private James Peter Robertson, the last of nine Canadian VC recipients during the battle of Passchendaele. Robertson volunteered for the task of silencing a German machine gun that was wreaking havoc on the 27th Battalion. Robertson charged the post, killed four Germans with his bayonet and turned the machine gun around on the remainder of the fleeing soldiers. While carrying the machine gun he led a charge into Passchendaele. Once they had returned to their own lines, they realized two wounded comrades had been left behind. Robertson immediately returned and rescued the first soldier, but was fatally hit by an exploding shell while carrying the second wounded soldier to safety.

Touring the Amiens battlefields

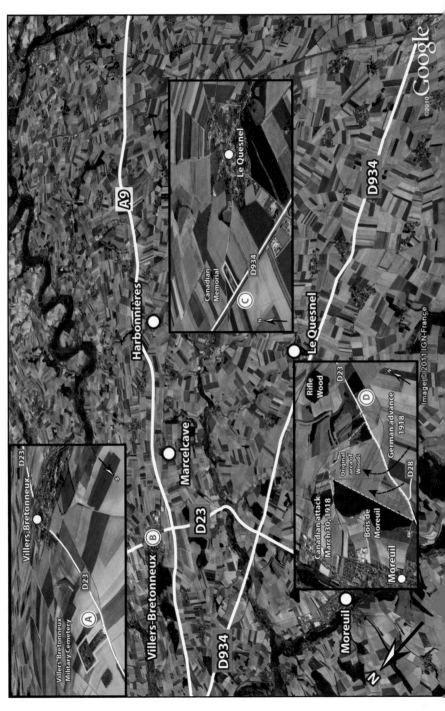

Touring Amiens

To do justice to the Amiens offensive allocate a day to your tour of the area. You might begin or end the day at the cathedral in Amiens, one of the glories of Western civilization (GPS – 30 Place Notre Dame, Cathédrale, 80000 Amiens, France). Apart from the scale of a Gothic cathedral large enough to hold several Notre Dames, four-hundred carved figures adorn the church with some of the most amazing stained glass windows in France. A number of plaques commemorating regiments and events, especially related to the defence of the city during the German offensive of 1918, hold a prominent place.

If you wish to stay in Amiens there are a number of good hotels and exceptional restaurants. We have stayed in the Best Western L'Univers, an older establishment with comfortable rooms. The Holiday Inn Express and the Carleton are also possibilities but the new Mercure beside the cathedral should be your first choice.

 Begin the battlefield tour at the Australian Memorial near Villers-Bretonneux (GPS – Route de Villers Bretonneux 80800 Fouilloy, France). From Arras make your way to the D265/N25 towards Doullens where you follow the N25 South to Amiens. Wrap east around the city on the N25 and exit on the D1029 toward Villers-Bretonneux. Turn left on the Rue de Corbie and the memorial will be on your right. The cemetery in front of the memorial contains the graves of 266 Canadians including Jean Brillant of the 22nd Battalion.

The gravestone of Jean Brillant, Victoria Cross recipient. [Nick Lachance]

A view from the tower at the Australian National Memorial. [Matt Symes]

Brillant, who had previously won the Military Cross, won the Victoria Cross during the battle of Amiens. On 8 August 1918, near Méharicourt in France, Brillant singlehandedly neutralized a machine gun position that was holding up the advance of the left flank. Despite being wounded he remained in command and the next day led two platoons against the enemy position when the advance once again stalled. The success of the attack led to the capture of fifteen machine guns and 150 enemy soldiers but Brillant was wounded again. Brillant then led another attack against a German position but this time was critically wounded and collapsed from exhaustion and loss of blood. His VC citation concluded that "Lt. Brillant's wonderful example throughout the day inspired his men with an enthusiasm and dash which largely contributed towards the success of the operation."

There are also 779 Australians buried at Villers-Bretonneux and the memorial lists the names of the 10,700 Australians who have no known grave – a sobering sight. The memorial tower provides an exceptional overview of the Australian sector and the left flank of the Canadian advance. The view is well worth the climb – bring your binoculars.

B There is a small Franco-Australian Museum in Villers-Bretonneux, open daily except Sundays (GPS – 9 Rue Victoria, 80800 Villers-Bretonneux, France). Retrace your steps to Villers-Bretonneux and continue south on the D23. Turn right onto Rue Droit. The museum is located in an old schoolhouse that was originally a gift of Australian school children to the youth of Villers-Bretoneux in honour of the Australian war dead in the area. While much of the commemoration following the First World War featured monuments like Vimy and Thiepval, this schoolhouse bears many similarities to the "progressive" memorials of the Second World War that used the sacrifice to construct something of meaning for future generations like hospitals, parks, and schools. For more information on the museum visit www.museeaustralien.com. You may also wish to visit the striking Australian Monument at le Hamel, the site of the major Australian victory that influenced the plan for the Amiens offensive.

C The D23 which runs south from Villers-Bretonneux is the quickest route to the D934 and the Canadian Memorial at Le Quesnel (GPS – D934 80134 Le Quesnel, France will put you at the intersection of the D41 and D934. Continue on the D934 towards Amiens and the monument is on your right). From Villers-Bretonneux make your way south on the D23. Turn left on the D934. You will have to make a U-turn once you reach the D41 as the memorial is on the

The Canadian Memorial at Le Quesnel. [Eric McGeer]

opposite side of the divided highway. The tour map illustrates the routes to the villages that figure in the narrative of the battle but there is little to see except rich farming country, pastoral scenery and pleasant villages. The bridge over the River Luce and the old D934, called Rue du Pont, is barely discernible and it is hard to imagine a 200 metre-wide marsh instead of reclaimed farm land. The villages of Hangard, Démain, and Courcelles were rebuilt after the war. Marcelcave is larger and boasts a (reconstructed) 16th century church of some note as well as a striking Great War monument.

D In a static war where the Cavalry was made redundant by trenches and modern weaponry, the village of Moreuil and the nearby woods were the scene of history's 'Last Great Cavalry Charge' led by the Fort Garry Horse, the Royal Canadian Dragoons and Lord Strathcona's Horse (GPS – D23, 80110 Moreuil, France). Continue toward Amiens on the D934 and take a left heading south on the D23. 1.3 kilometres toward Moreuil you are on the northeast tip of the original battlefield. Farm fields now occupy what used to be the middle section of Moreuil Wood which originally extended to the D23. Pull over before you reach the fork with D28 and the battlefield is on your right. This gives you a commanding view of the battleground from the German perspective. Moreuil Wood was a labyrinth of saplings, heavy undergrowth and Ash trees not yet in

Sir Alfred Munnings, *Charge of Flowerdew's Squadron*. [CWM 19710261-0443].

bloom in March 1918 which created treacherous conditions for riding. Orders were to delay the German advance as much as possible. The Fort Garry Horse was sent to protect the village. After being driven back on their first attempt, the Royal Canadian Dragoons and elements of Lord Strathcona's Horse dismounted, entered the wood and engaged the enemy in vicious hand to hand combat. Lieutenant Gordon Flowerdew, the Commander of 'C' Squadron discovered two German lines of infantry positions supported by machine guns and ordered the charge. The cavalry passed over both of the lines, killing many Germans. Flowerdew then led his men over the lines again, which caused the enemy to break and run. The cost was heavy with more than 70 percent of 'C' squadron killed or wounded, including Flowerdew who had been shot through both thighs. Those left manned the former enemy positions and held them overnight. It is perhaps ironic that the 'Last Great Cavalry Charge' was made possible by a greater number of dismounted cavalry engaged in close combat. Flowerdew died the next day from his injuries and the Germans soon recaptured and held Moreuil Wood until August.

Canadians interested in the 'Last Great Cavalry Charge' will want to continue slightly past Amiens to Namps-au-Val Cemetery where Gordon Flowerdew is buried (GPS – Derrière les Haies 80710 Namps-Maisnil, France). Flowerdew was born in Billingford, Norfolk and emigrated to British Columbia to take up ranching. When war broke out in 1914 he joined Lord Strathcona's horse and rose through the ranks to command 'C' Squadron just before the action at Moreuil Wood. There are several other Commonwealth War Cemeteries in the area and those interested should consult Norm Christie's guidebook *The Canadians at Amiens* or the Commonwealth War Graves Commission website.

TOUR

Touring Arras to the Canal du Nord

Touring Arras and Cambrai

(A) The start line for the "Battle of the Scarpe" was located just west of the A1 autoroute. Leaving Arras on the D393 heading to Cambrai you may wish to explore the ground over which Third Division advanced to seize Monchy-le-Preux from the north. Turn left at the traffic circle signed D37 then left again onto the Rue de Feuchy. The road lies close to the start-line of the 8th Canadian Infantry Brigade. It is worth the trip to Orange Hill Cemetery to gain an overview of the position attacked frontally by 5th CMR while 4th CMR worked its way around the main defences before striking south towards Monchy (GPS – Chemin des Revers 62217 Tilloy-lès-Mofflaines, France). Orange Hill Cemetery is one of the smallest Commonwealth cemeteries with 42 Canadian graves and 1 British grave, including a number of Canadian Mounted Rifles (CMR).

(B) Return toward the D939 and turn left on Boulevard d'Europe and follow the road directly to Monchy-le-Preux. As you enter the village on the Rue de Tilleul look back towards Orange Hill and Arras. In the centre of town, the memorial to the Royal Newfoundland Regiment and the monument to the British 37th Division are of special interest (GPS – 1-5 Rue de la Chaussy 62118 Monchy-le-Preux, France).

The Newfoundland Memorial at Monchy-Le-Preux. [Matt Symes]

Third Division, with Brutinel's Brigade and the Cyclist Battalion on their left flank, advanced to Jigsaw Wood, Boiry-Notre-Dame, and Vis-en-Artois, breaking through the Fresnes-Rouvray Line before handing over control to 4th British Division. To view this optional part of the tour take Rue de Vis southeast to the D34 and turn left toward Boiry-Notre-Dame. Both villages were reduced to ruins before September 1918 and both have been rebuilt largely on their original sites. For those who can read enough French to get by, the Mairie (the Local mayor's office) in Boiry sells two booklets on the history of the village; one on the First World War that includes information on the reconstruction, and one on the occupation in the Second World War (GPS - La Place de Lamotte 62156 Boiry-Notre-Dame, France).

(C) From Monchy, take the D33 south to D939 east to the Vis-en-Artois British Commonwealth Cemetery (GPS – 1 Route Nationale 62156 Haucourt, France). Among the original 430 graves in Plot I and II there are 297 Canadians. Now, there are 2,342 burials here including 582 Canadians. This is also the site of the Memorial to 9,822 British and South African soldiers who were killed between 8 August 1918 and the Armistice and have no known grave.

To visit the Second Division battlefields, drive west on the D939 to the road signed "Guemappe" (about two kilometres). Turn left on the D34. The village was seized by the 4th Brigade in the initial attack. Continue through Guemappe to a junction and go left to Wancourt in 5th Brigade's sector. The 27th and 28th Battalions had been ordered to turn south to support the British Third Army's stalled advance, capturing Wancourt and pressing forward to the Wancourt Tower located on a low ridge east of the village.

Turn left at the main crossroads in Wancourt, pausing at the British Cemetery which has 246 Canadian burials from 1918 (GPS – 1 Rue d'Alsace 62128 Wancourt, France – the Cemetery is visible on the right from this point). You are now in the centre of the division's battlefield. The remains of the Wancourt Tower are at the next crossroads. This was the start line for 5th Brigade's attack towards Chérisy.

(D) Georges Vanier, who later became Canada's Governor-General, lost his leg in this action. Many of his comrades are buried at the Quebec

Quebec Cemetery. [Nick Lachance]

Cemetery which is located in the middle of a farmer's field outside of Chérisy (GPS – D38 62128 Chérisy, France - from here head southeast and take your second left). From the cemetery in Wancourt take Rue d'Alsace south to Chérisy. The cemetery, which is the final resting spot of more than 189 Canadians, is complicated to find. Leave Chérisy on the D38 heading southeast. Take your second left and the cemetery is on your left well into the field. It is worth the walk.

The First Division relieved the Second before the final assault on this section of the Fresnes-Rourray Line began. Though there is nothing to see, the village of Hendencourt-lès-Cagnicourt is within Third Army's sector. To follow this portion of the battle take the D38 south from Chérisy. The division broke through north of Hendecourt, paralleling the advance of 4th Canadian Division astride the Arras-Cambrai road.

(E) All of this was in preparation for the set-piece attack on the D-Q Line. The D956 from Hendecourt to Dury crosses the line just south of the D939. Return to the Arras-Cambrai road to visit the Canadian Memorial (GPS – D939 62182 Dury, France). The Dury Canadian Memorial, one of the eight sites selected by the Canadian Battlefield Monuments Commission, is on the north side of the highway and is clearly signed with a parking space. The inscription reads:

Touring The Canal du Nord and Cambrai

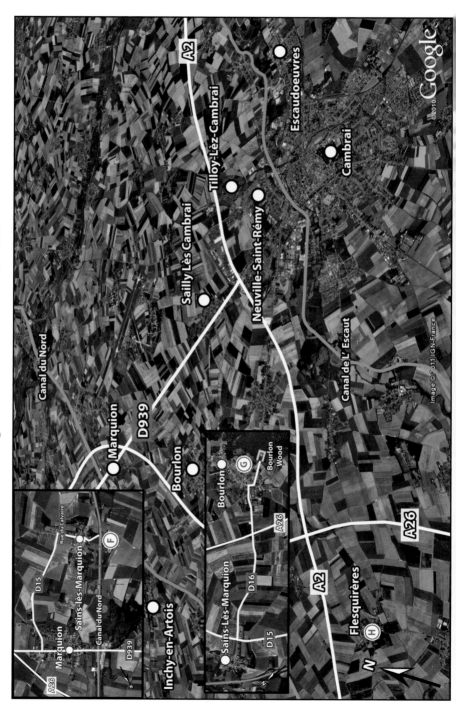

The Canadian Corps, 100,000 strong, Attacked at Arras on August 26th 1918. Stormed Successive German Lines and Here on September 2nd Broke and Turned the Main German Position on the Western Front and Reached the Canal Du Nord.

(F) There are no signs of the trenches or barbed wire that marked the Drocourt-Quéant Line and considerable imagination is needed to relate photographs from 1918 to the pastoral landscape before you. Continue east on the D939 crossing the Canal du Nord, turning right on the D15 to Sains-lès Marquion (GPS – 2 Rue de Baralle 62860 Sains-lès-Marquion, France – when you re-cross the canal watch for the dirt road on your right). You are also in the area of the left flank of the Canadian sector where First Division crossed what was then an incomplete, dry canal.

Terry Copp explains the crossing of the Canal du Nord. [Nick Lachance]

While you are near Sains-lès-Marquion you may wish to visit Ontario cemetery which is 1.6 kilometres south of the village on the D15. A large portion of the 257 identified men buried there are from to the Second, Third and Fourth Battalions all raised in Ontario. The original 144 burials are from the fighting for Sains-lès Marquion, the rest were gathered from battlefields and German graveyards after the Armistice (GPS – D15 62860 Sains-lès-Marquion, France).

(G) Follow the D16 toward Bourlon Wood (GPS – 15-17 Avenue du Bois 62860 Bourlon, France). The route to the Canadian Memorial is well marked at the end of Avenue du Monument. The memorial is located at the top of a stunning set of terraces. The stairs to the memorial are lined with the original shell shattered ancient lime trees that were nursed back to health after the war. Don't miss Bourlon Wood.

The Canadian Memorial at Bourlon Wood. [Matt Symes]

Leave Bourlon on the Rue de la Gare returning to the D939 which became the boundary between First and Third Army in the battle for Cambrai. The Canadians as First Army's right flank Corps advanced on the north side of the highway through the Marcoing Line and on towards the Canal de l'Escaut through Sailly-lès-Cambrai, Tilloy and Neuville-Saint-Rémy. Cambrai was finally captured on 9 October when Second Canadian Division crossed the Canal de l'Escaut, seizing the village of Escaudoeuvres and advancing to meet 24th British Division to complete the encirclement. The Third Canadian Division entered the city crossing the canal just north of the D939 or Route d'Arras. The D630 will take you through Neuville-St.Rémy and Escaudoeuvres but there is little to see. (GPS – 18-26 Rue du Pont Rouge 59554 Neuville-Saint-Rémy, France). Cambrai itself was heavily damaged but the central area has been rebuilt.

(H) Most military tourists will be interested in the well-preserved Mk IV tank "Deborah D51" that was unearthed at Flesquières (www.tank-cambrai.com). From Cambrai take the D630 south west and then take a left on the D15 heading south. At Havrincourt veer left on Rue des Calettes and then left

Deborah D51 at the Cambrai Tank Museum. [Alex Groarke]

again on the D92/Rue Neuve which takes you directly to Flesquières. Deborah was part of the attack on the Hindenburg Line when it was put out of commission by enemy fire. Four of the eight man crew survived and made it back to their own line, an action that earned Second Lieutenant Frank Heap the Military Cross. When the Allies took control of the ground, the damaged tank was placed into a hole originally dug by the Germans with the intent of building a concrete bunker. The tank was used as a shelter by the British. Contact visite.org@tank-cambrai. com to arrange a visit.

Maurice Galbraith Cullen, *The Cambrai Road*. [CWM 19880266-002]

Touring Valenciennes to Mons

Touring Valenciennes to Mons

Following the Canadians' advance to Mons and finishing with a visit to St. Symphorien Cemetery is the classic end of the First World War tour, however the journey is long and only for the devoted battlefield tourist. Mons is less than an hour's drive from Cambrai on the autoroute but in 1918 the advance began on 12 October and ended a month later with the Armistice. If you work your way across country over the Canal de la Sensée through Demain and the Forêt de Raimses, pausing in Valenciennes to plan a set-piece attack from Mont Houy into the heart of the city, some of the difficulties of the last month of the war would become evident.

A To retrace the path of 4th Division in the Battle of Valenciennes, exit the A2 autoroute (Exit 21A) south on the D958 towards Famars. At the roundabout take the third exit onto the D288 and Mont Houy is to your right (GPS – D288 59300 Famars, France). Return to the D958, which becomes Avenue Georges Pompidou. Valenciennes is a busy town of 40,000 which on the whole

German POWs taken during the Hundred Days Campaign.

prefers to forget the years of German occupation and the destruction of parts of the city during the battle.

(B) Those interested in the conscription crisis will want to visit the St. Roch Cemetery which contains the graves of 151 Canadians including many conscripts (GPS – 103 Avenue Duchesnois 59300 Valenciennes, France).

Mons

Return to the A2, which becomes A7, to reach the main square in Mons where the war ended (GPS – Grand'Place 22 7000 Mons, Belgium). Mons is "Bergen" in Flemish, both names remind us of the hill that marks the town. The main square, le Grand Place, and the town centre are organized to keep car traffic to a minimum. If you are staying in Mons choose a hotel with on-site parking close to the city centre. The Grand Place and nearby streets are lined with restaurants in all price ranges. If you are not staying in Mons you might want to avoid the city centre.

Sir Arthur Currie congratulates Canadian troops in Mons.

(C) The last Allied soldier killed in the war, Canadian Private George Price of the 28th Northwest Battalion, is commemorated by a plaque and a footbridge over the canal which carries his name (GPS – Rue de Mons 2597070 Le Roeulx, Belgium). To get to the walking bridge from the A7, exit onto the B501 and follow it to the R50. Take a left on the R50 continuing around the edge of Mons and take a left onto the N90. From the N90 take a left on the N538/

Inglis Harry Jodrel Sheldon-Williams, *The Return to Mons*. [CWM 19710261-0813]

Chassée du Roeulx. Continue on N538 and cross the waterway parallel to the walking bridge on your right. Take your first left toward Ville-Sur-Haine on the N552. Take your first left onto Rue de Mons and the monument is at the foot of the walking bridge at the end of the street. Price, a 25-year-old from Nova Scotia, was killed by a sniper on 11 November 1918 while searching a house that had been used by German machine gunners. The plaque was originally unveiled on the 50th anniversary of the Armistice by his former comrades on the house where Price died. Widening of the canal led to the destruction of the farmhouse where Price's fellow soldiers tried in vain to keep him alive but the plaque is surrounded by the bricks from the original structure.

(D) Price's grave, as well as those of the first and last British soldiers killed in the Great War, can be found at St. Symphorien Cemetery (GPS – Rue Nestor Dehon 7030 Mons, Belgium). Retrace your steps back to

Mons and when you reach the N90 go east. Follow the N90 east until the roundabout in St. Symphorien and take the first right onto the N564. The well-marked cemetery is about one kilometre down the road. This joint British and German cemetery was constructed by the Germans in 1914. An obelisk erected by the German Army in memory of the German and British soldiers who died near Mons in 1914 dominates the scene. Look for the grave of John Parr, a 16-year-old cyclist scout and the first British casualty of the war. Facing Parr is the grave of George Ellison, the last of almost 900,000 British war dead. In many ways the death of Private George Lawrence Price at 10:58am on 11 November 1918 epitomizes the calamity of the Great War. He was the last soldier killed in a four year conflict that counted almost ten million total war dead including more than 5.5 million Allied casualties. With a population of just over 7.5 million and a mobilized force of more than 620,000, Price was the last of more than 65,000 Canadians and 1,305 Newfoundlanders killed in the "war to end all wars."

Mary Riter Hamilton, *Comrades*. [LAC 1988-180-122]

A SOLDIER
OF THE GREAT WAR
5TH BN: CANADIAN INF.

KNOWN UNTO GOD

There could be no truer measure of the impact of the First World War and its shocking death toll than the efforts made to commemorate the fallen. More than a thousand war cemeteries cluster along the old Western Front, while no fewer than seventeen memorials listing the names of the missing stand in mute testimony to the destructive power of the Great War. One hundred and fifty war cemeteries dot the landscape in the Ypres Salient, two hundred and forty house the dead on the Somme battlefields – each of the battlefield tours will lead you past these "silent cities," and the monuments preserving the memory of Canada's efforts and sacrifice in the Great War. We have therefore included two appendices outlining the Canadian battlefield memorials and the principles which guided the design and construction of the Commonwealth war cemeteries.

The Brooding Soldier. [Matt Symes]

Official First World War Canadian Memorials

The Canadian Battlefields Memorial Commission (CBMC) was established in 1920. Based on the recommendations of senior officers the Commission selected eight sites (listed below) on which to commemorate the achievements of Canadian soldiers in the Great War. The CBMC launched a national architectural and design competition in December of 1920 and out of the 160 submissions chose seventeen finalists who were then asked to produce a plaster maquette of their design. There was some indecision at first, as it was unclear whether the CBMC wanted eight identical monuments or wished to give certain battles greater significance; but eventually, as Jonathan Vance has noted, "in many ways the outcome of the CBMC's deliberations was governed by the designs submitted...two stood far above the others." What became known as the Brooding Soldier, proposed by Regina sculptor Frederick Clemesha, was selected for St. Julien. What became Canada's most famous war memorial, the twin pylons atop Vimy Ridge, was the creation of Toronto artist Walter Allward. The remaining six locations received identical granite block monuments (each with an inscription commemorating the relevant feat of arms) which were to be placed on a low circular flagstone terrace within a small landscaped park.

CBMC design competition plaster maquettes of finalists in the competition. [VA]

Canadian Memorials in Belgium

St. Julien – commemorating the heroic stand of the First Canadian Division during the gas attack at Ypres in April 1915.

Hill 62 – commemorating the part played by Canadian troops in the defence of Ypres between June and August 1916.

Passchendaele – commemorating the capture of Crest Farm by the Canadian Corps during the Battle of Passchendaele, October-November 1917.

Canadian Memorials in France

Courcelette – commemorating the part played by the Canadian Corps in forcing the Germans back from their defences on the Somme from September to November 1916.

Vimy – commemorating the capture of Vimy Ridge by the Canadian Corps on 9-12 April 1917.

Le Quesnel – commemorating the attack by the Canadian Corps, 100,000 strong, on 8 August 1918, which drove the enemy back a distance of eight miles on the first day and commenced the triumphant advance of the Hundred Days.

Dury – commemorating the capture of the Drocourt-Quéant Switch and the breaking of the Hindenburg Line on 2 September 1918, during the Second Battle of Arras.

Bourlon Wood – commemorating the crossing of the Canal du Nord, the apture of Bourlon Wood, and the rupture of the final Hindenburg Line defences on 27 September 1918.

Some of the most striking monuments on the Western Front, featuring the caribou symbol of the Royal Newfoundland Regiment, honour the distinct contribution made by Newfoundland to the Allied cause:

Newfoundland Memorials in Belgium

Courtrai (Kortrijk) – commemorating the performance of the Royal Newfoundland Regiment in the Battle of Lys in October 1918.

The Vimy Memorial. [Matt Symes]

Newfoundland Memorials in France

Beaumont-Hamel – commemorating the sacrifice made by the Royal Newfoundland Regiment in the Battle of the Somme on 1 July 1916.

Gueudecourt – commemorating the successful action of the Royal Newfoundland Regiment in the Battle of the Somme on 12 October 1916.

Monchy-le-Preux – commemorating the Newfoundlanders' participation in the Battle of Arras on 14 April 1917.

Masnières – commemorating the participation of the Newfoundland Regiment in the Battle of Cambrai on 20 November 1917.

The official unveiling of the Monument at Beaumont-Hamel, June 7, 1925. Field Marshall Sir Douglas Haig and French General Marie Fayolle were in attendance and visible in the photo. [NAS (130)X234011]

Commonwealth War Cemeteries

The Imperial War Graves Commission (the Commonwealth War Graves Commission since 1960) was established in 1917. The Commission was responsible for the identification and burial of the war dead of the British Empire, and to maintain the cemeteries and memorials in perpetuity. At the behest of Sir Frederic Kenyon, director of the British Museum, three of the greatest architects of the time, Sir Edwin Lutyens, Sir Herbert Baker, and Sir Reginald Blomfield, worked out the standard design and features for the war cemeteries. One of the most gifted writers in the English language, Rudyard Kipling, was invited to compose the commemorative formulae appropriate to the monuments and headstones. Amidst much deliberation and debate – some of it quite heated, especially on the choice of religious imagery, the use of a headstone as opposed to a cross, and the policy that the dead not be repatriated for private interment but buried among their comrades in the lands where they had fallen – the Commission's guiding principles were laid out in Kenyon's 1918 report:

1. Each of the dead should be commemorated individually by name on a headstone or on a memorial dedicated to the missing.

2. Headstones and memorials should be permanent.

3. Headstones should be uniform in design and the inscription of personal details.

4. There should be no distinction made on account of military or civil rank, race, or creed (although the Commission took great care to observe the traditions of non-Christian or Jewish peoples, such as the Hindus, Sikhs, and Muslims of the Indian Army, or the Chinese who served in labour battalions).

Visitors to the war cemeteries will notice great variety within the uniformity of monumental features. Small battlefield cemeteries may hold as few as forty or fifty burials, where the vast collection cemeteries, such as Etaples or Tyne Cot, contain 11,000 and 12,000 respectively. The cemetery names preserve the names of the old Western Front (Cheddar Villa, Ration Farm, Stump Road) and sometimes the nicknames bestowed by homesick soldiers (Lancashire Cottage,

Caesar's Nose, Dud Corner, or the immortal puns on Flemish place names, Bandaghem, Dozinghem, Mendinghem, i.e. "bandage 'em," "dosing 'em," and "mending 'em"). Dominion Cemetery, Toronto Avenue Cemetery, Maple Leaf Cemetery, Quebec Cemetery are a few examples of the names attesting to the Canadians in a given sector.

The cemeteries are usually enclosed by low brick walls and entered through wrought-iron gates, but there is no standard pattern for the interior. In most cases the architects sought to conserve the original outlay wartime burial grounds with their jigsaws of graves huddled around a former dressing station or aid post. Cemeteries with more than forty burials feature Sir Reginald Blomfield's Cross of Sacrifice (with an inlaid Crusader sword), the only overtly religious symbol common to the war cemeteries. Cemeteries with more than a thousand burials will also feature Sir Edwin Lutyens's deliberately neutral Stone of Remembrance, on which the words "Their name liveth for evermore" appear. They were proposed by Rudyard Kipling, who in his regard for the fallen and their families felt that no words of his own could do them justice, and so turned to chapter 44 of the Book of Ecclesiasticus. But as the father of a son listed among the missing, Kipling looked within himself to find the simple, moving formulation "A soldier of the Great War, known unto God," which visitors will see on nearly half of all graves.

The Stone of Remembrance and the Cross of Sacrifice. [Matt Symes]

The headstones over identified burials present the personal details in descending order: regimental insignia (on British graves) or national emblem (a maple leaf, for instance, on Canadian graves); enlistment number and rank; the soldier's name; his unit; date of death and age (if known). A Cross or Star of David was engraved below the register of personal information, but the religious symbol was omitted if the soldier's papers listed no religious affiliation or if his family forbade the inclusion of a religious symbol. For a small cost the families could also have a short valedictory inscription placed beneath the Cross: "Son of my heart, live forever. There is no death for you and me," "The only child of aged parents," "Death is not a barrier to love, Daddy," "The shell that stilled his true young heart broke mine. Mother" – many are indescribably moving and convey the sorrows of the parents, wives, and children, unknown to history, who bore the burden of loss imposed by the Great War for the rest of their lives.

Unlike the sombre French or German cemeteries, the Commonwealth war cemeteries present the aspect of an English cottage garden, in keeping with Kenyon's assertion that "there is no reason why cemeteries should be places of gloom." With this in mind, the architects worked closely with leading horticulturalists to blend flowers and plants native to England with local varieties

Canadian war dead buried behind the lines near a dressing station, May 1916. [PA 000176]

and to offset the uniformity of white monumental features with the colours of nature. The perfectly manicured lawns and constant maintenance added to the impression of a carefully tended garden that despite its solemnity could become a place of renewal and even hope. In a gesture of reconciliation, German burials were often included in the Commonwealth cemeteries. As the cemeteries took shape during the 1920s and the monuments were raised in honour of the fallen, many felt the sorrow and desire of King Edward VIII as he told a Canadian mother at the unveiling of the Vimy Memorial, "Pray God, madam, it shall not happen again." Sadly and ironically, however, just as the Commission's work was nearing completion in the late 1930s, the Great War resumed in a far more terrible form.

Today more than 900 gardeners tend to the cemeteries of both World Wars. The lawns, plants, and flowers are groomed and replaced when necessary, as are the headstones which the elements have worn or effaced. Five percent of a cemetery is redone each year, so that the whole is redone every twenty years. The bodies of soldiers killed nearly a century ago still emerge from the battlefields, and the Commission makes every effort to identify them, give them an honoured burial, and to contact next of kin. For more information, visit the Commonwealth War Graves Commission website (www.cwgc.org).

Ontario Cemetery. [Matt Symes]

Online Resources

The Internet offers many opportunities to enrich our understanding of the war and the sites of memory in France and Belgium. Search engines will offer many choices and you will no doubt explore the options on your own, but you might wish to start with www.firstworldwar.com, "a multi-media history of World War One." Almost everything on this site is worth exploring. Click on "Battles" then "Western Front" for excellent, brief descriptions of specific actions. Be sure to listen to the original wartime music in the "Vintage Audio and Video" section. The personal stories in "Memoirs and Diaries," "War in the Air," and "Primary Documents" are all of great interest. Paul Reed's "Battlefields 1918" is an excellent source for photos and maps. www.WW1battlefields.co.uk is aimed at assisting those who tour the actual battlefields. Canadian sites, including Essex Farm, Courcelette, Beaumont-Hamel, are included. The Commonwealth War Graves Commission's website, www.cwgc.org, helps you to locate the graves of individual soldiers. There are brief histories of the main battles and an image browser with photos from the Imperial War Museum. Check the BBC website for World War One. The text offers a revisionist "the war was a remarkable victory" narrative reflecting the views of a group of British historians.

Canadian sites to consult include the audio/visual material at Veterans Affairs Canada (www.veterans.gc.ca/remembers), the Canadian War Museum (www.warmuseum.ca), the Maple Leaf Legacy Project (www.mapleleaflegacy. ca), and King and Empire (www.kingandempire.com) which has an easy to use set of links to other websites. The attestation papers for over 600,000 First World War soldiers, nurses, and chaplains are instantly available online at the Library and Archives Canada (http://www.collectionscanada.gc.ca/databases/cef/index-e.html). The Canadian War Museum offers its own introduction to the First World War including many teacher resources (http://www.warmuseum.ca/cwm/exhibitions/guerre/home-e.aspx). The CBC archives (archives.cbc.ca) is a treasure trove of excellent First World War audio/visual sources including video and radio clips during the war and also the many specials the broadcasting corporation has aired since. As of January of 2009, the National Film Board (www.nfb.ca) has been releasing videos for Canadians to stream online free. If you use the search feature in the top right corner and enter "First World War" you will have a number of documentaries to select from. Last, but not least, check our Centre's website www.canadianmilitaryhistory.ca for links to materials related to this and other guidebooks and publications.

List of Websites as they Appear in the Guide

www.historial.org

www.mapleleaflegacy.ca

www.greatwar. co.uk

www.somme-trench-museum.co.uk

www.somme-battlefields.com.

www.carriere-wellington.com

www.passchendaele.be

www.museeaustralien.com.

www.tank-cambrai.com

www.cwgc.org

www.firstworldwar.com

www.WW1battlefields.co.uk

www.cwgc.org

www.veterans.gc.ca/remembers

www.warmuseum.ca

www.nfb.ca

www.kingandempire.com

www.canadianmilitaryhistory.ca

Alfred Bastien, *Scottish Canadians in the Dust*. [CWM 19710261-0067]

Terry Copp is a long-serving and charismatic professor at Wilfrid Laurier University and the founder of the Laurier Centre for Military Strategic and Disarmament Studies. Copp is the leading scholar of Canada's military role in World War II and an influential advocate for military history in both military and civilian post-secondary education. His work on battle exhaustion, published in 1990; his study, *The Brigade* (1992); and his two important volumes on the Canadians in Normandy, *Fields of Fire* (2003) and *Cinderella Army* (2006), have led to a reinterpretation of Canadian soldiers' effectiveness in 1944 and 1945. Copp's interest in the battlefields of Northwest Europe has also led to the creation of battlefield memorials, the conduct of tours for teacher and students, and the publication of invaluable battlefield guides to Canadian participation in both world wars. He is the founder of a quarterly journal published by the Laurier Centre in co-operation with the Canadian War Museum; entitled *Canadian Military History*, it is Canada's leading journal of military history.

Matt Symes is a PhD candidate at Wilfrid Laurier University. He works as the Publications Manager for the Laurier Centre for Military Strategic and Disarmament Studies and the Online Editor for canadianmilitaryhistory.ca. With Eric McGeer, Matt has published three Battlefield Guides on the Italian Campaign in the Second World War. With Geoff Hayes and Mike Bechthold, he is the Co-editor of *Canada and the Second World War: Essays in Honour of Terry Copp* (Forthcoming WLU Press 2012).

ADDITIONAL INFORMATION

Nick Lachance is a mature student finishing his BA in Honours History at Wilfrid Laurier University. As a research assistant at LCMSDS he manages the digitization of the 300,000 Second World War aerial reconnaissance photographs the center has in its possession. A freelance photographer and photojournalist, many of Lachance's photos appear in this and other LCMSDS publications. Nick currently freelances as a photojournalist with long-term plans to attend Loyalist College to study photojournalism.

A Note on Photo References

COHC references refer to the Canadian House of Commons Archive.

GDHI references refer to images from the German Archives.

IWM references refer to the Imperial War Museum.

NAS reference refer to images from The National Archives of Scotland.

PA references refer to images from the Library and Archives Canada.

PANL references refer to the Public Archives of Newfoundland and Labrador.

ZK references refer to images from the Canadian Forces Joint Imagery Center.

Photos Without Captions

p. 7 - Tank at Amiens. [PA 3667]

p. 93 - The Brooding Soldier. [Nick Lachance]

p. 119 - The Mourning Mother - Wikimedia Commons, The Mourning Father - Wikimedia Commons, Truth and Knowledge - Geoff Keelan, Mother Canada - Matt Symes, The Spirit of Sacrifice and Passing of the Torch - Nick Lachance, The Stone Sarcophagus - Nick Lachance, The Wall of Defence - Nick Lachance, The Breaking the sword - Wikimedia Commons, Sympathy of the Canadians for the Helpless - Wikimedia Commons.

p. 145 - The grave Private Price. [Matt Symes]

p. 147 - A Soldier of the Great War. [Matt Symes]